THE EMPIRE STRIKES BACK SKETCHBOOK

# INTRODUCTION

Joe Johnston, Art Director of Special Effects on THE EMPIRE STRIKES BACK, and his assistant, Nilo Rodis-Jamero, are the artists responsible for the sketches in this book.

Johnston was originally hired by Lucasfilm in 1975 to be storyboard artist for STAR WARS. Once those storyboards were developed, Johnston was asked to sketch the various spacecraft appearing in the climactic Death Star battle scene. Many of these imaginative and detailed sketches, which were used as blueprint guides by the model makers, may be found in THE STAR WARS SKETCHBOOK (Ballantine Books, 1977).

For THE EMPIRE STRIKES BACK, the sequel to STAR WARS, Johnston's creative role was expanded to include not only the storyboard designs, but also scene layouts, shot designs and compositions, miniature designs, and all special effect sequences as they related to the film.

Again, his designs were used as guides to the model makers after first being approved by George Lucas. Guided by the principle that modifying the drawings would be easier than altering a model, Johnston and Lucas met frequently to work out the concepts for the new EMPIRE characters and vehicles before the models were built. These new concepts included the snow walker, Rebel Cruiser, snowspeeder, Yoda, and Boba Fett.

Collaborating with Johnston on the realization of some of these designs, Nilo Rodis-Jamero assisted in developing many of the concepts for the spacecraft and other vehicles. In addition, Rodis-Jamero drew half of the storyboards, assisted in modifying vehicle designs, helped build the prototype snow walker model, and was responsible for the design, construction, and coordination of the miniature sets for THE EMPIRE STRIKES BACK. This meant that he was required to design sets that completely matched the location sets where the live-action shots were filmed.

Joe Johnston was raised in Texas and, when his family moved to Los Angeles, attended California State College in Long Beach where he majored in Industrial Design. He is now a resident of San Anselmo, California.

Nilo Rodis-Jamero studied Industrial Design at San José State College. After several years working as a designer of cars, boats, industrial vehicles, and military tanks, Rodis-Jamero joined Lucasfilm in the summer of 1978.

# THE EMPIRE STRIKES BACK™

## SKETCHBOOK

By
Joe Johnston
And
Nilo Rodis-Jamero

Art Director and Editor, Diana Attias
Research, Valerie Hoffman
Design, Ron Larson/Mike Donaldson

Ballantine Books – New York

Copyright © Lucasfilm, Ltd. (LFL) 1980

TM: A trademark of Lucasfilm, Ltd.

All rights reserved under International and Pan-American Copyright Conventions. Published in the United States by Ballantine Books, a division of Random House, Inc., New York, and simultaneously in Canada by Random House of Canada, Limited, Toronto, Canada.

Library of Congress Catalog Card Number: 80-66172

ISBN 0-345-28836-X

Manufactured in the United States of America

First Edition: June 1980

9 8 7 6 5 4 3 2 1

THE EMPIRE STRIKES BACK SKETCHBOOK

# GUN TURRETS ON HOTH

The turret design evolved from an early sketch of tanks in the snow. These tanks were outfitted with large, elongated turrets equipped with guns. But eventually George Lucas decided to use stationary gun towers, and Ralph McQuarrie developed the existing design.

REBEL GUN TURRET

REBEL/HOTH · GUN TOWER

THE EMPIRE STRIKES BACK SKETCHBOOK

# IMPERIAL PROBE DROID (Probot)

The buglike probe droid is an electronic Imperial scout, packed with supersensory surveillance equipment. The Imperial forces have hundreds of these probots which they dispatch from cruising Star Destroyers. Each of these robot spies is equipped with a laser gun for self-defense but, being expendable, can self-destruct if hit.

PROBOT

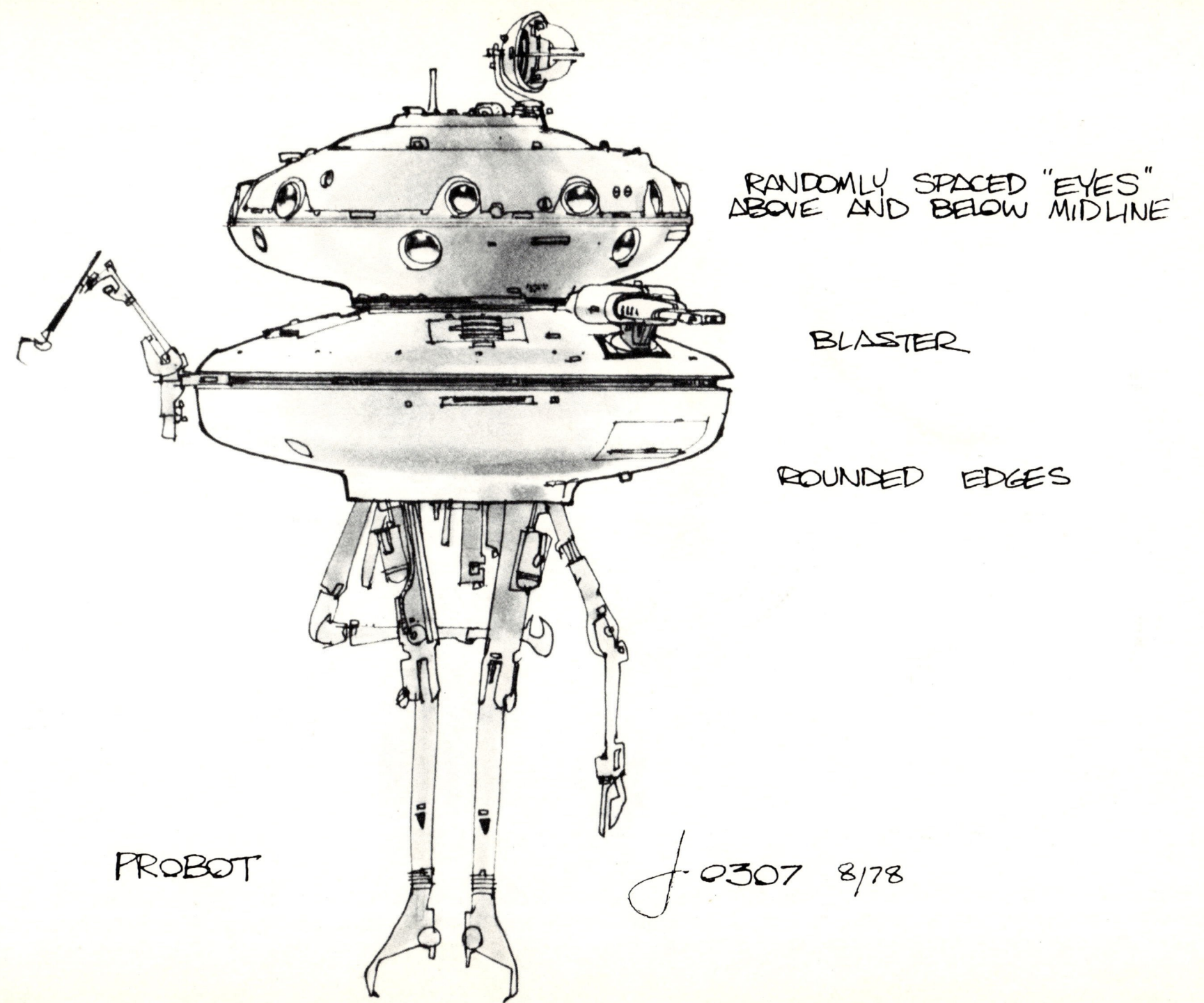

THE EMPIRE STRIKES BACK SKETCHBOOK

# REBEL ARMORED SNOWSPEEDER

The snowspeeder is a homemade military hot-rod, heavily armored, fast, and highly maneuverable. The basic "flying wedge" shape was first sketched by Ralph McQuarrie, and then Johnston did a mock-up and some sketches to define surface detail and to enlarge the craft to a two-man vehicle.

In the snow-battle sequence with the snow walkers, the speeders trip the slow-moving tanks by firing tow cables—to which are attached fusion discs—at the walkers, entwining the legs of the huge machines and tripping them when they attempt to move.

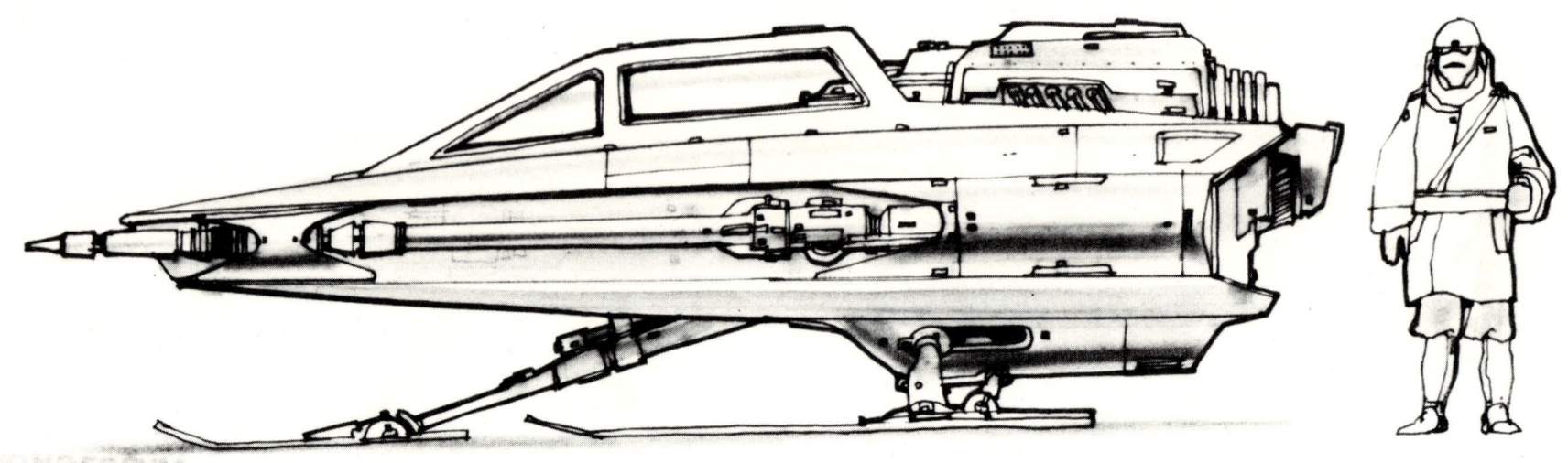
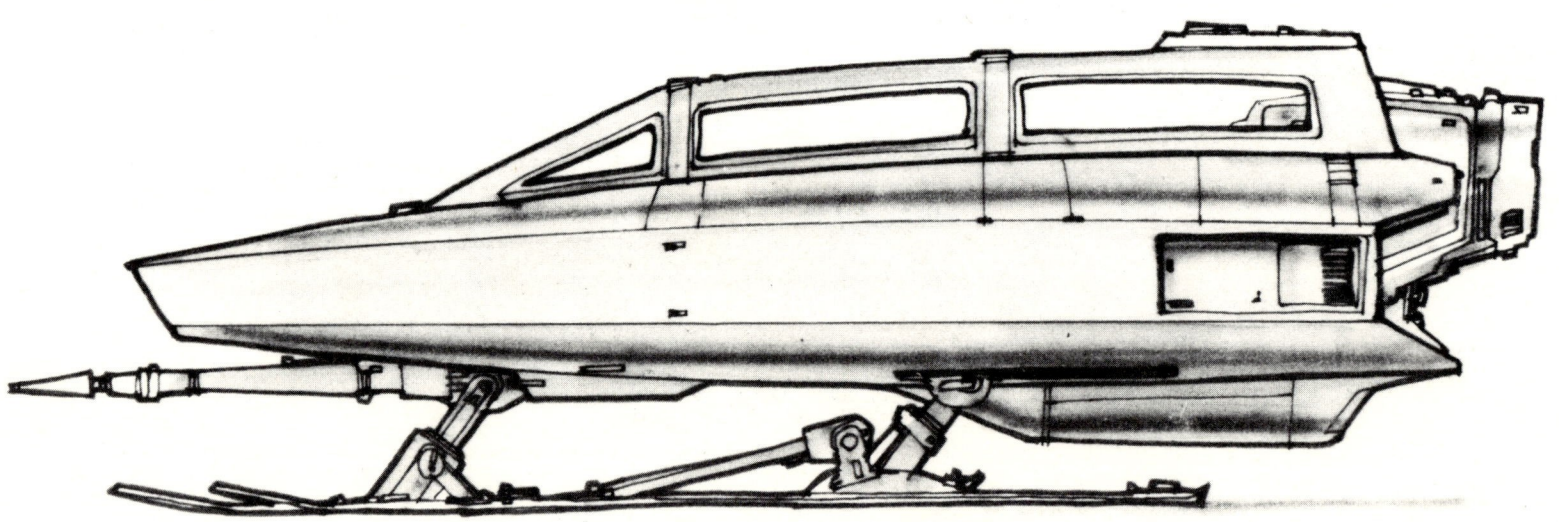

SIDE VIEWS OF EARLY SNOWSPEEDER DESIGNS

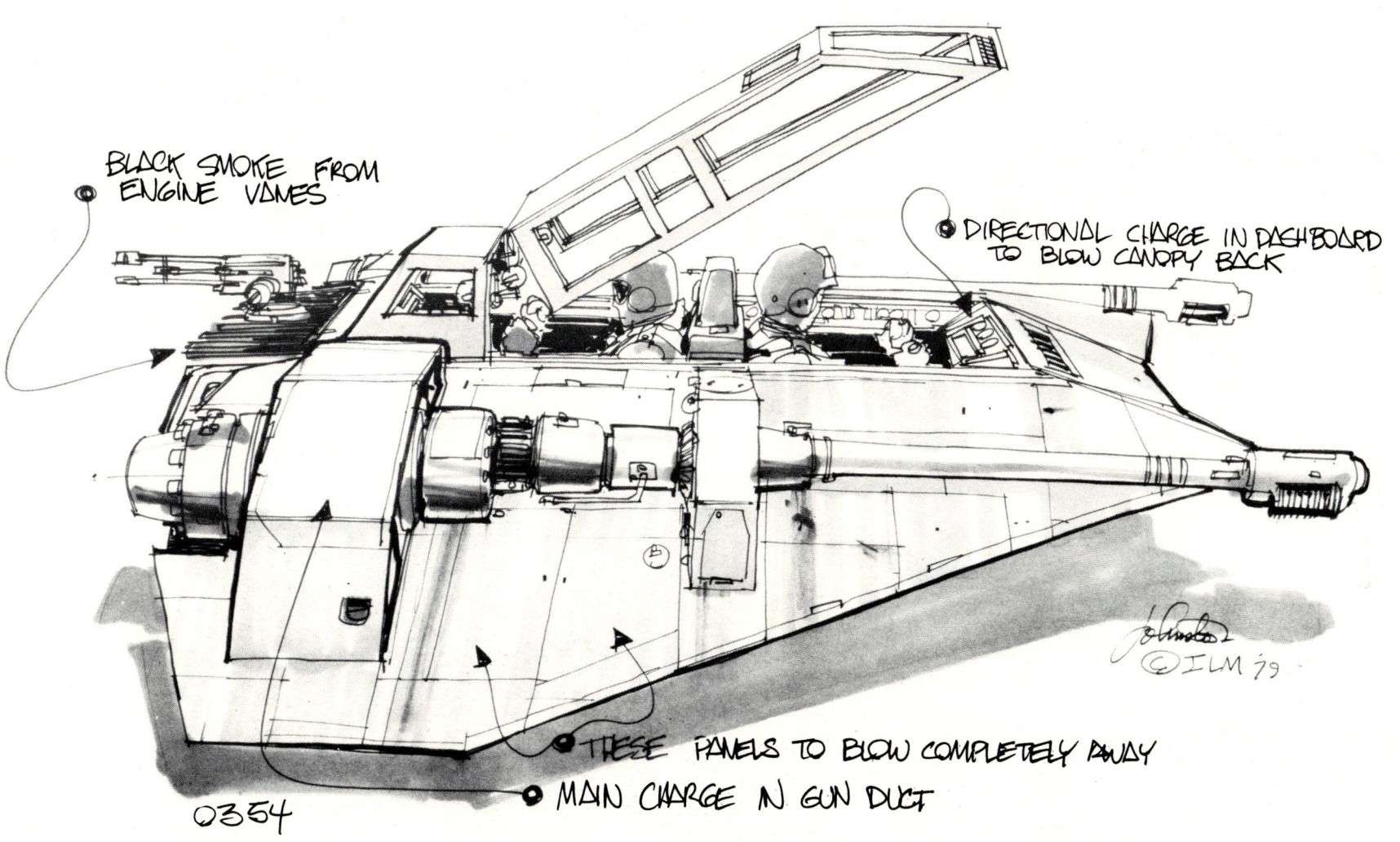

SNOWSPEEDER WITH INSTRUCTIONS FOR PYROTECHNICS

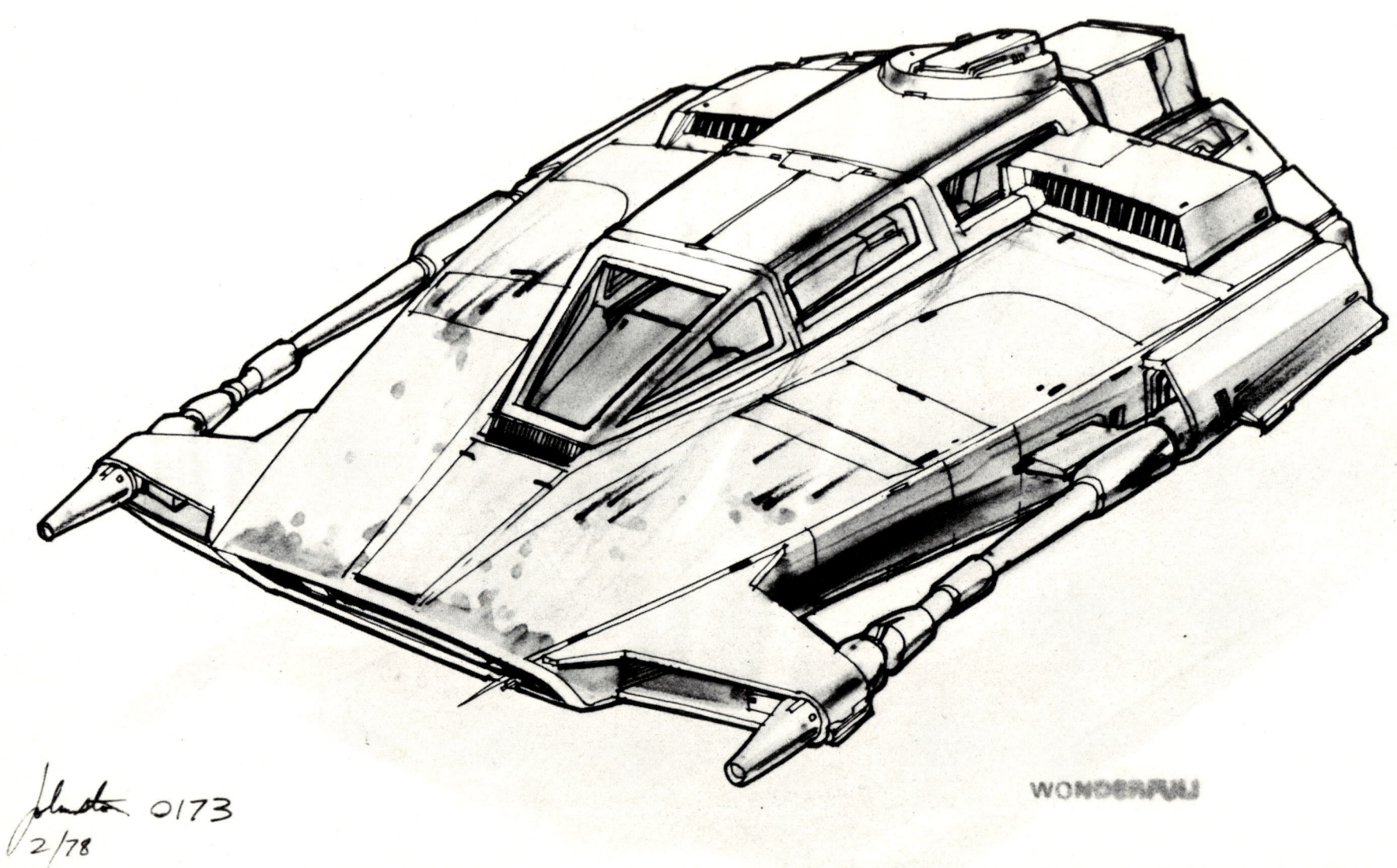

SNOWSPEEDER BUILT FROM MODIFIED Y-WING COCKPIT POD

REAR VIEW OF MODIFIED Y-WING SNOWSPEEDER

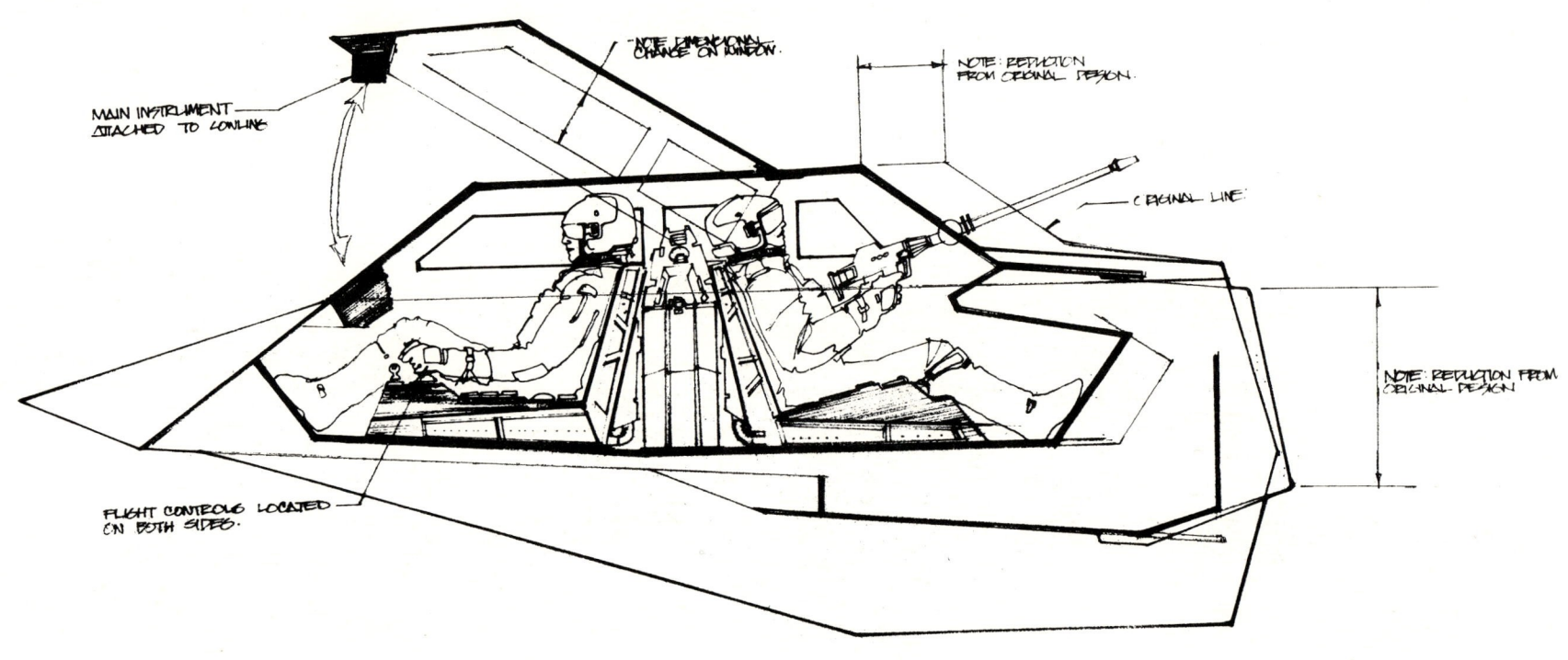

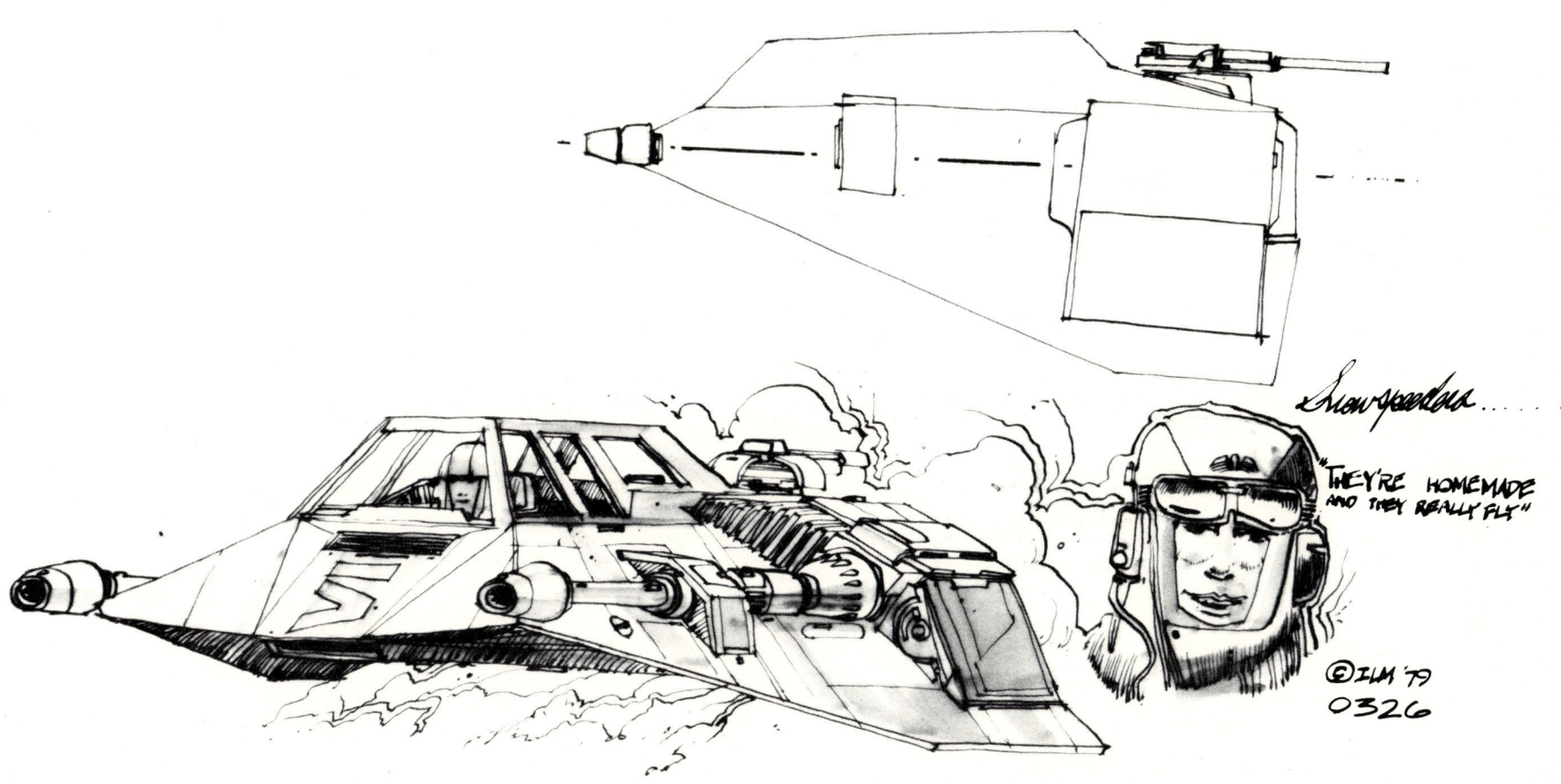

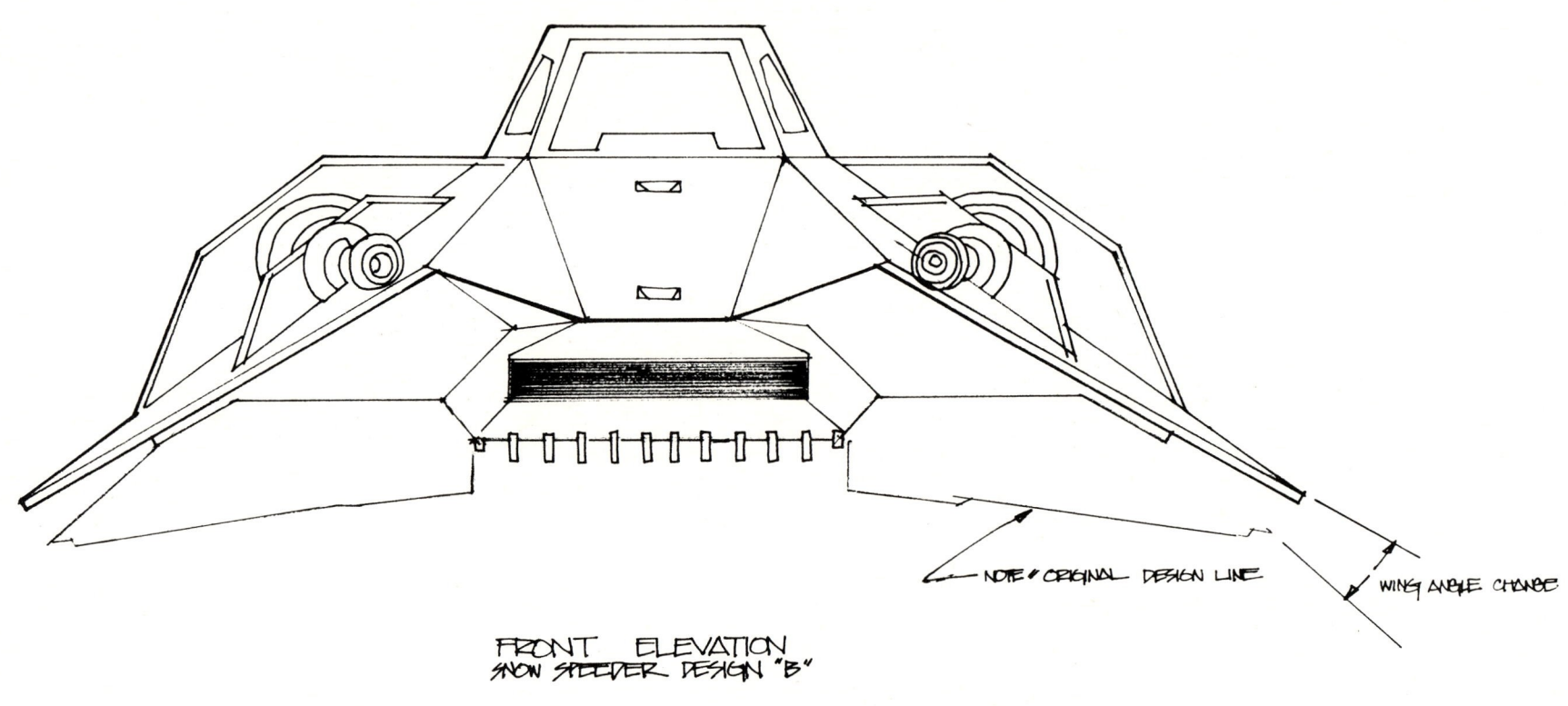

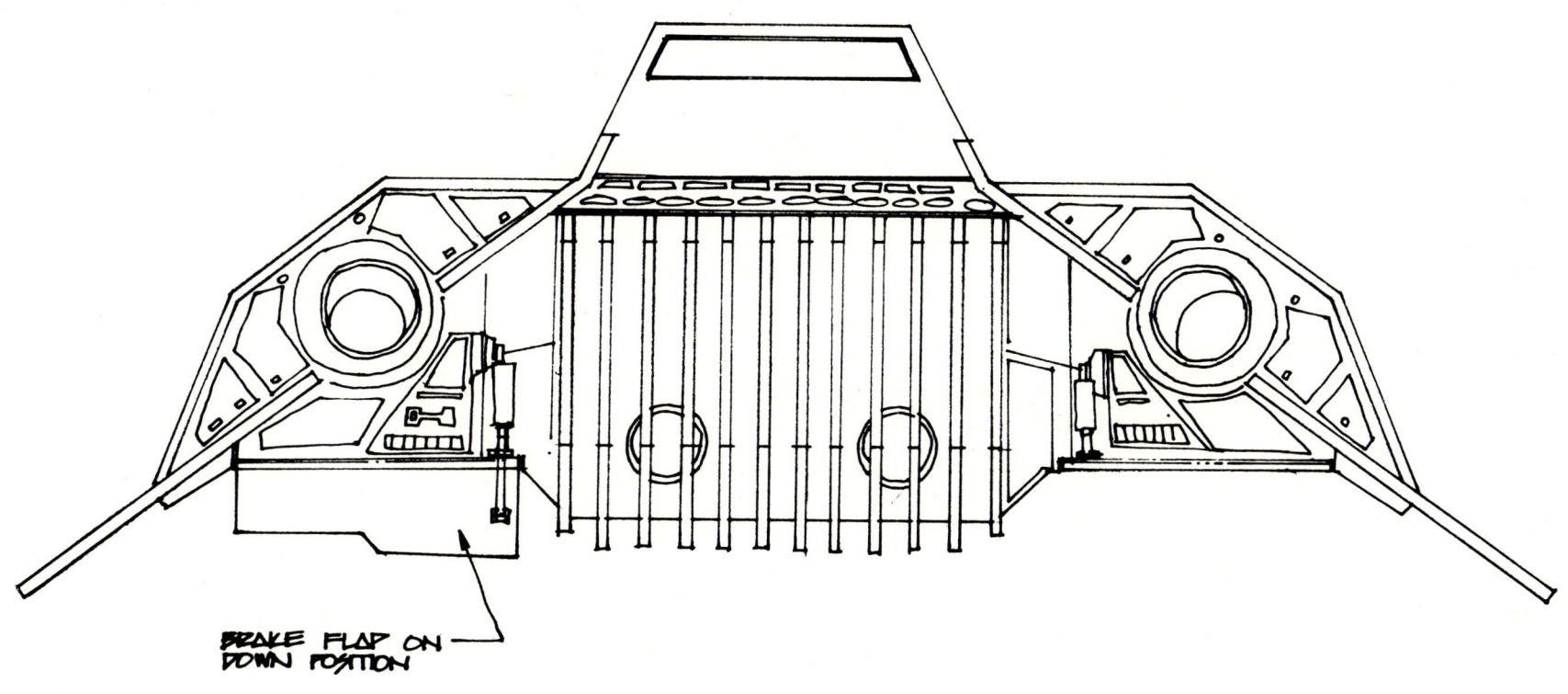

THE EMPIRE STRIKES BACK SKETCHBOOK

# SCOUT WALKER

The two-legged scout walker is a faster and lighter version of the giant snow walker. The scout walker holds one man and is used to reconnoiter positions for the main Imperial attack group. Lightly armed, the scout relies primarily on its speed and maneuverability for defense.

In the film, the model is animated in the same fashion as the snow walker.

VERY EARLY DRAWING OF SCOUT WALKER

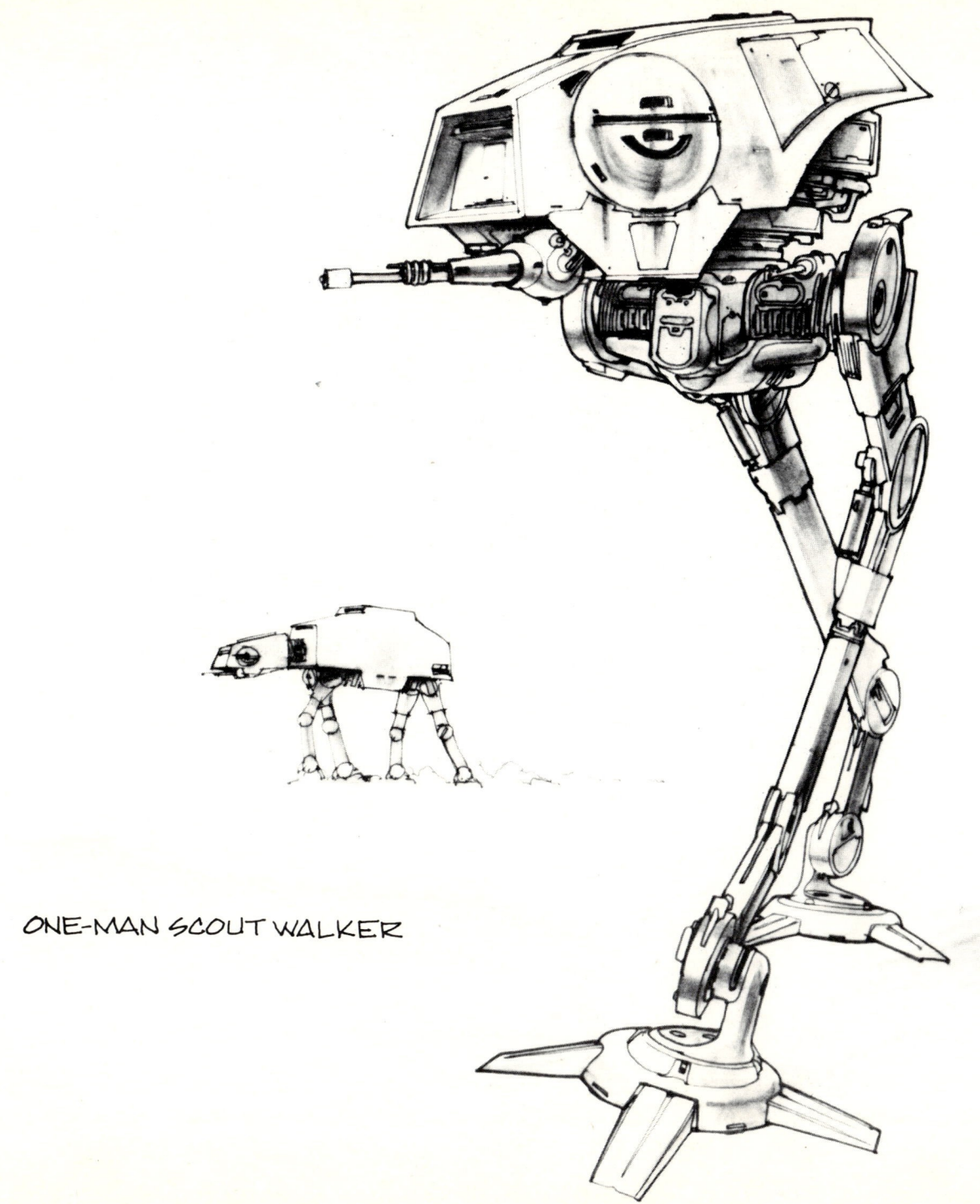

ONE-MAN SCOUT WALKER

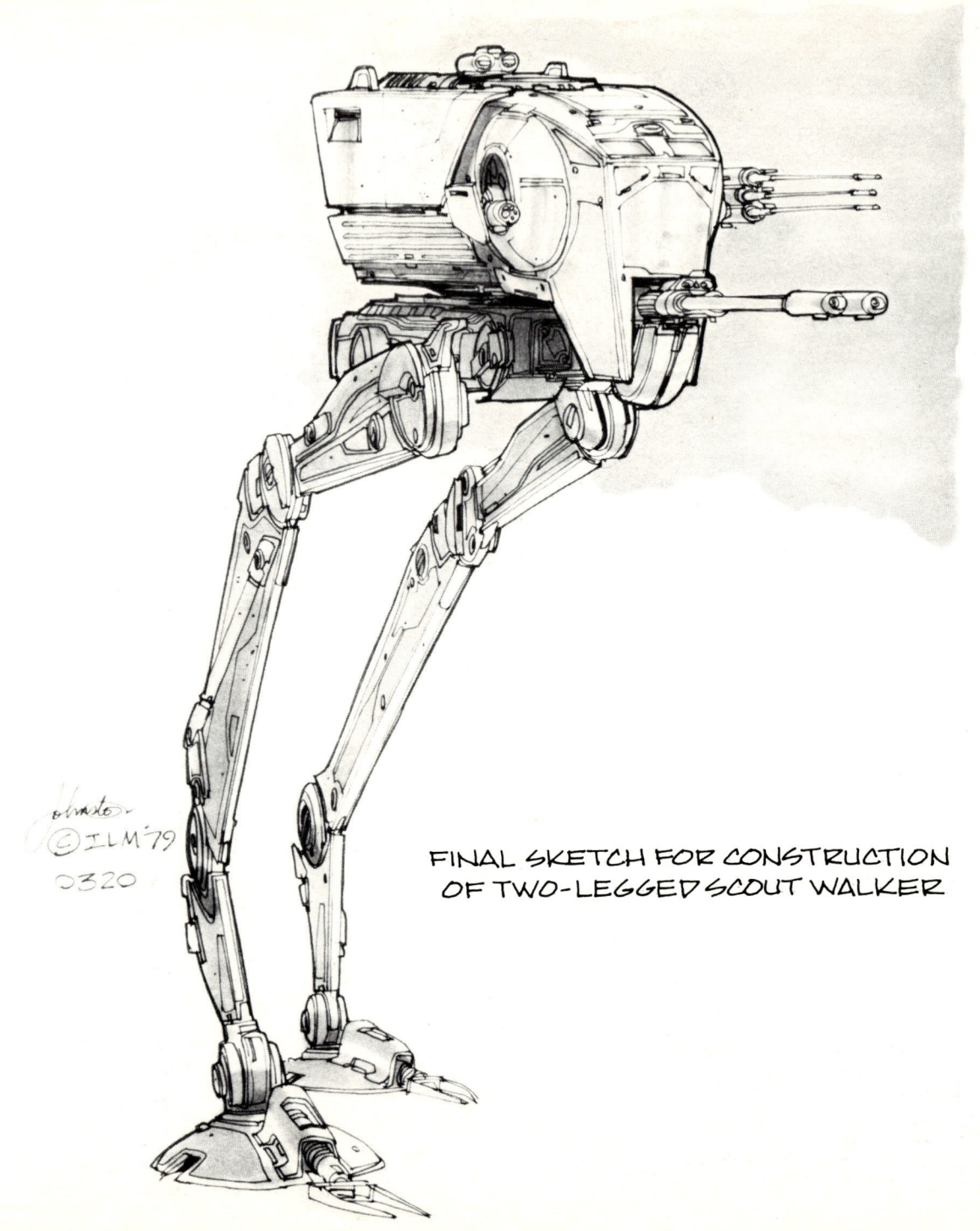

FINAL SKETCH FOR CONSTRUCTION OF TWO-LEGGED SCOUT WALKER

FINAL SKETCH FOR SCOUT WALKER

# SNOW WALKER (All Terrain Armored Transport; AT-AT)

The artists militarized a basic walking machine concept by giving it an armored body and guns, and designed a head that could turn as if seeking prey, an effect that lent animal characteristics to the walking tank. It was felt that the snow walker would be a much more awesome weapon if it were made to seem animallike, designed by the Imperial forces to terrify the enemy.

The walker interior was designed around the idea of two pilots and possibly one officer working inside the cockpit. A tight-fitting room, the cockpit would also house various controls and other hardware items needed to operate the complicated tank. Two operators were required to handle the two main lasers, two side guns, visions in the front, and the four walking legs.

Except for the set pieces needed for extreme closeups of the walker's underside and cockpit interiors, no full-size construction was necessary.

An eighteen-inch model of the machine—meant to appear fifty feet tall in the film—was built and used in stop-motion animation.

The model was set up on a miniature snowscape and shot a frame at a time as the legs were moved by very small increments between frames. The walker's mechanical nature made it an ideal subject for stop-motion work, as this sort of animation gives an unavoidable strobing effect. This effect lends a mechanical appearance to animal puppets, but only served to enhance the menacing movement the filmmakers wanted to achieve.

In devising movements for the walker miniatures, animators Jon Berg and Phil Tippett studied the movements of a variety of animals. But the walker's unique mechanism and design dictated its own movements.

PRE-WALKER TANK IDEA FOR IMPERIAL SNOW TROOPS

EARLY WALKER BODY AND HEAD

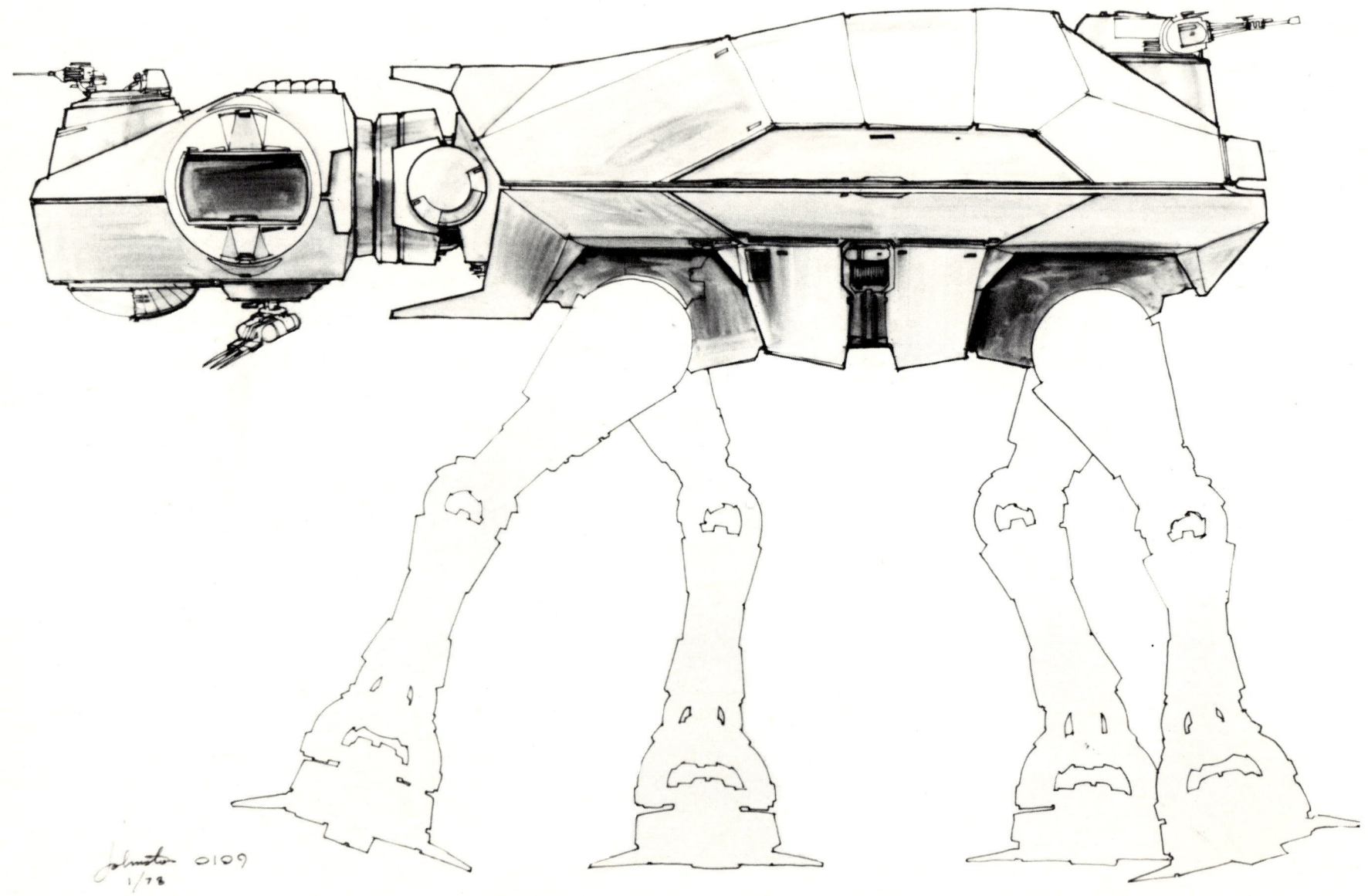

EARLY SKETCH OF "TURTLESHELL" WALKER BODY

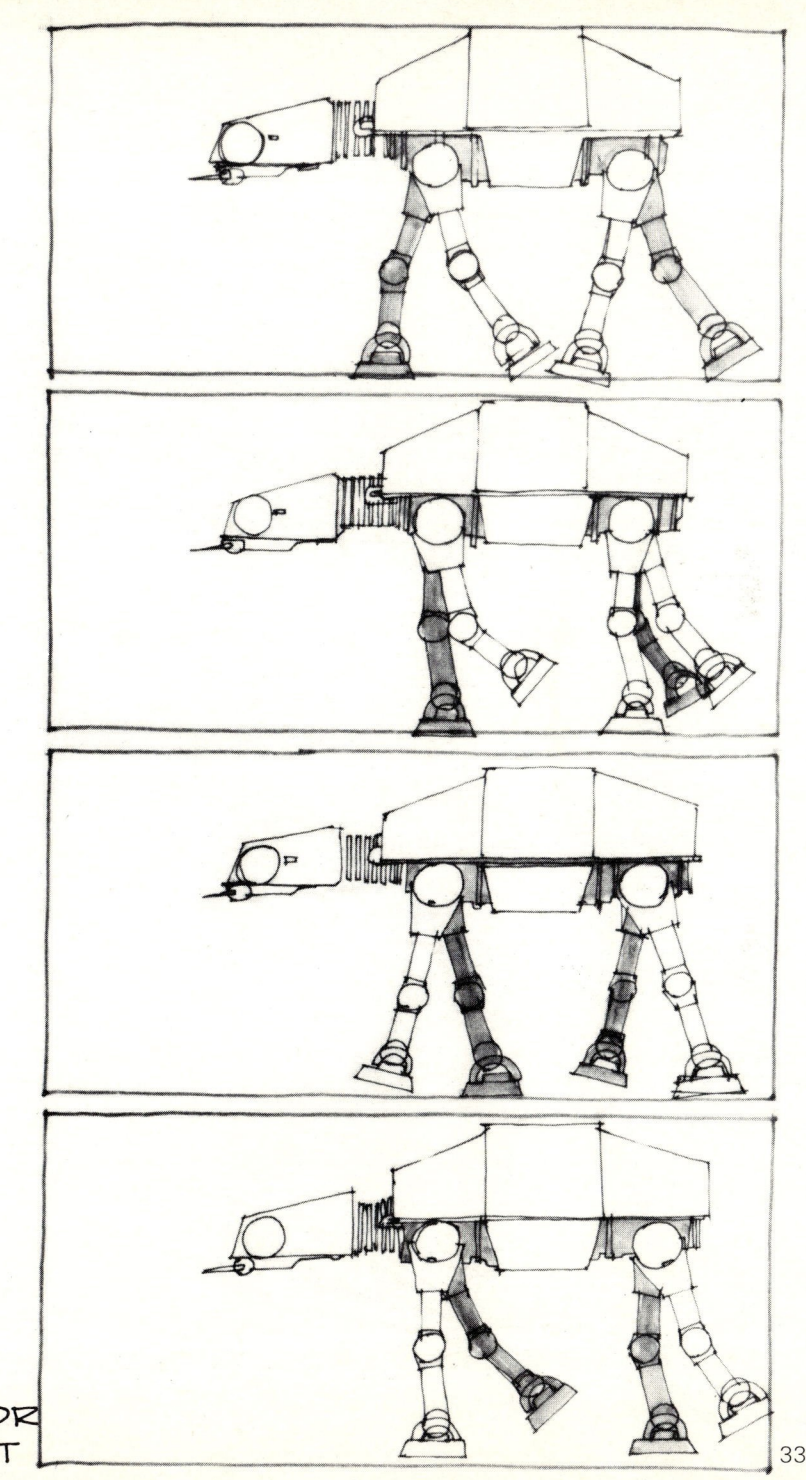

SEQUENTIAL SKETCH FOR
WALKER MOVEMENT

EARLY SKETCH OF WALKER FOOT WITH SNOWTROOPERS FOR SCALE

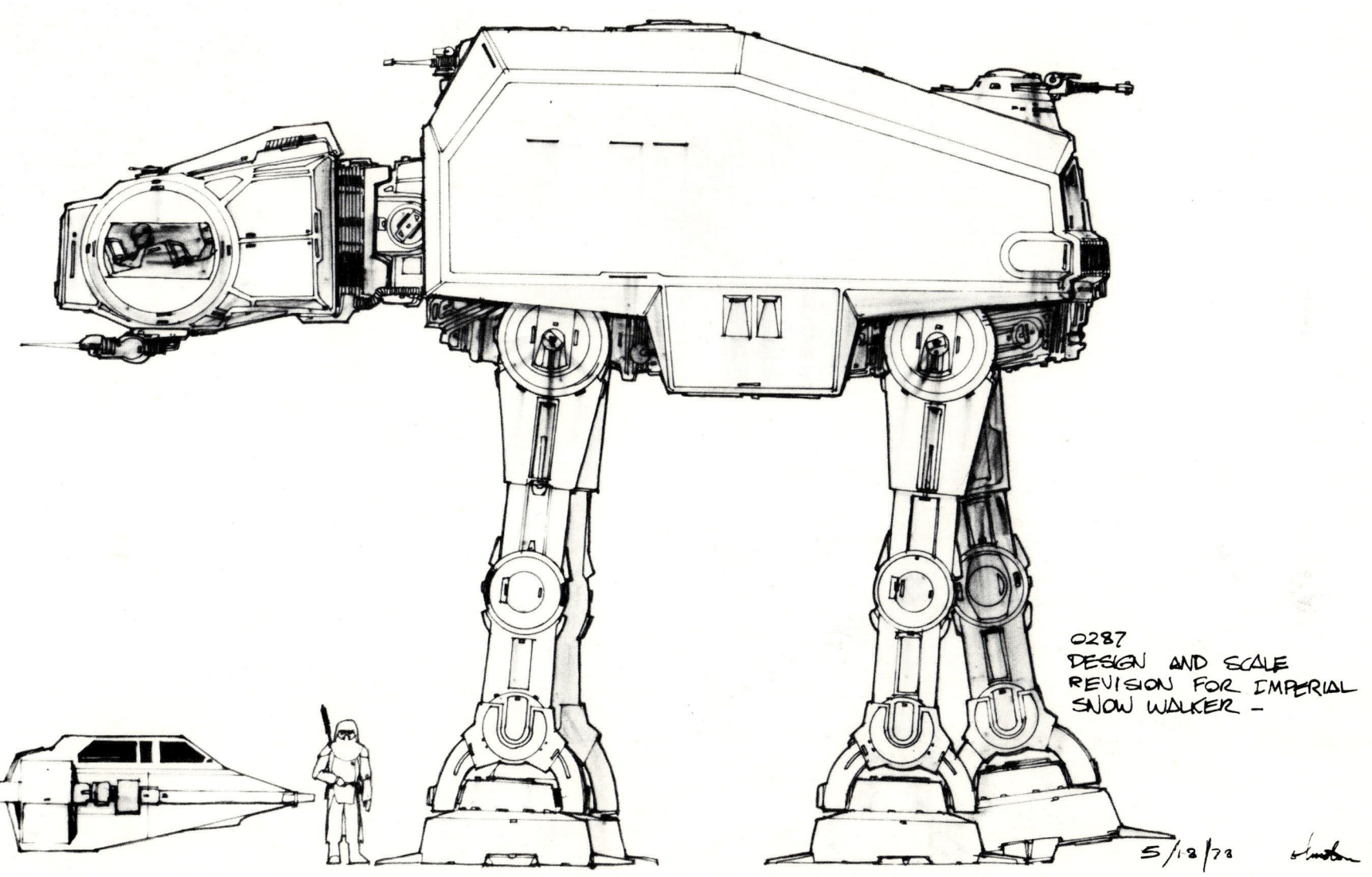

SKETCH WITH SNOWTROOPER AND SNOWSPEEDER TO SHOW WALKER SCALE

SNOW WALKER COCKPIT

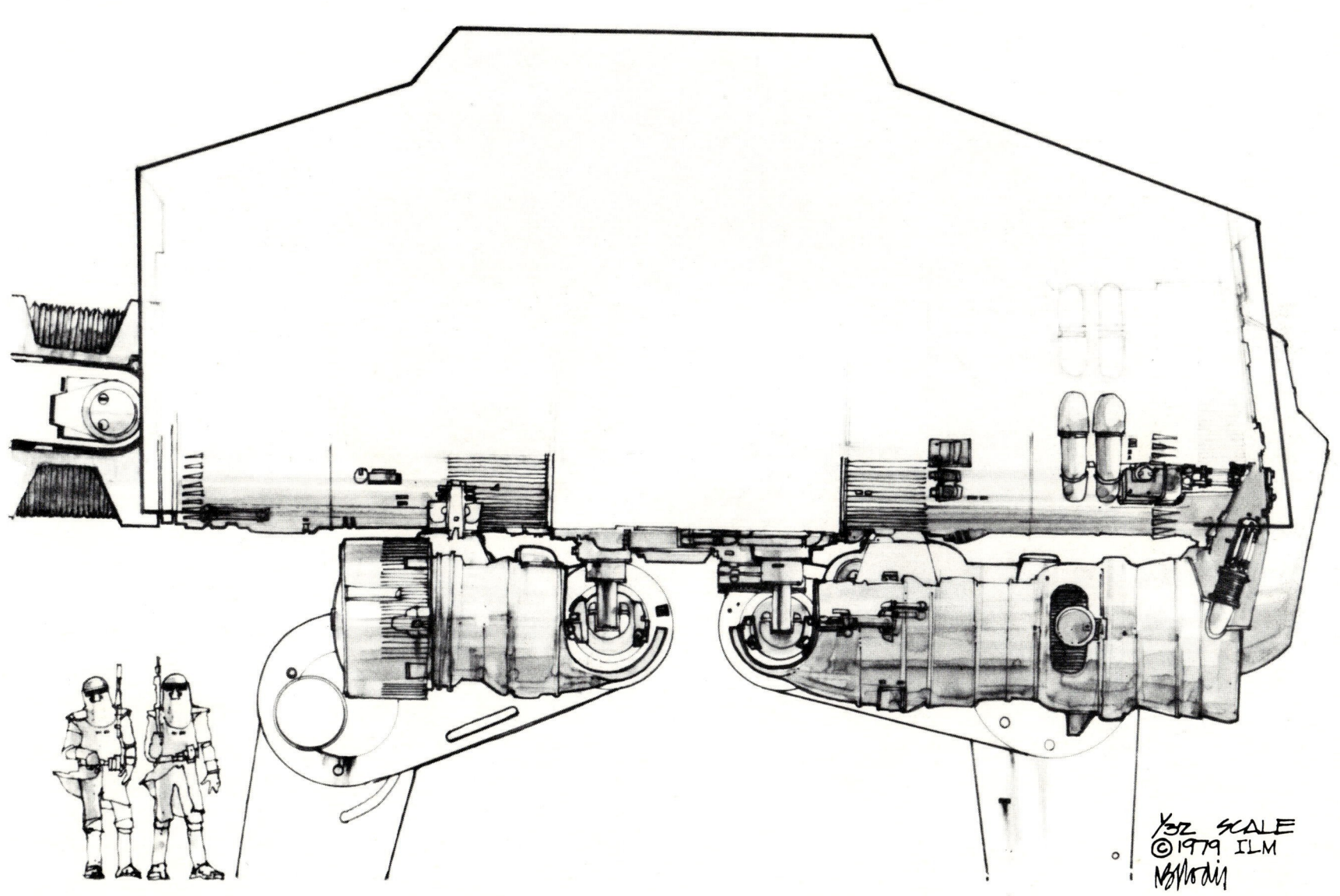

ENGINE DETAIL OF SNOW WALKER

FALLEN WALKER. REBEL P.O.V.

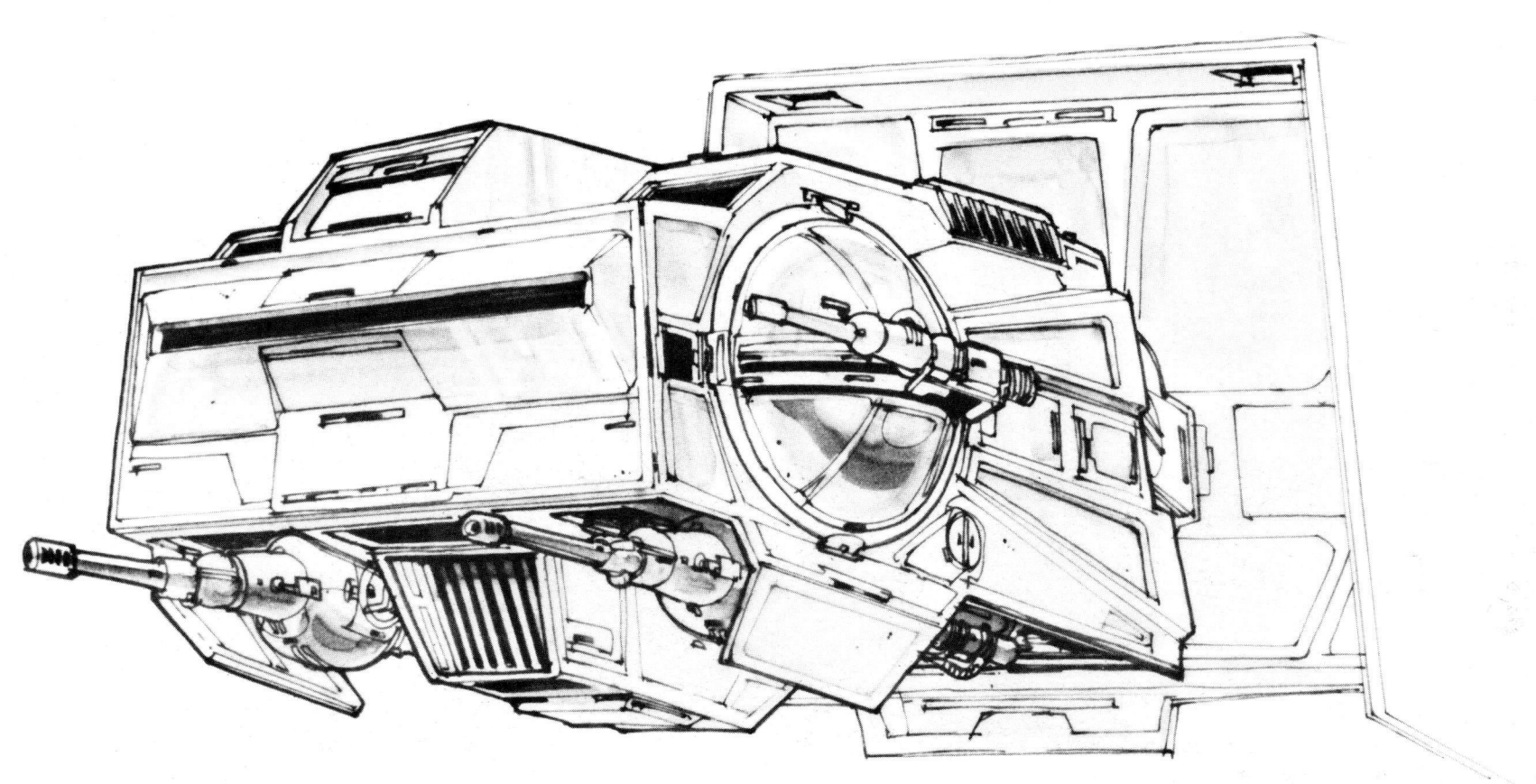

DEVELOPMENTAL SKETCH      HEAD OF IMPERIAL SNOW WALKER #1 - 0310
                                                       11-16-78

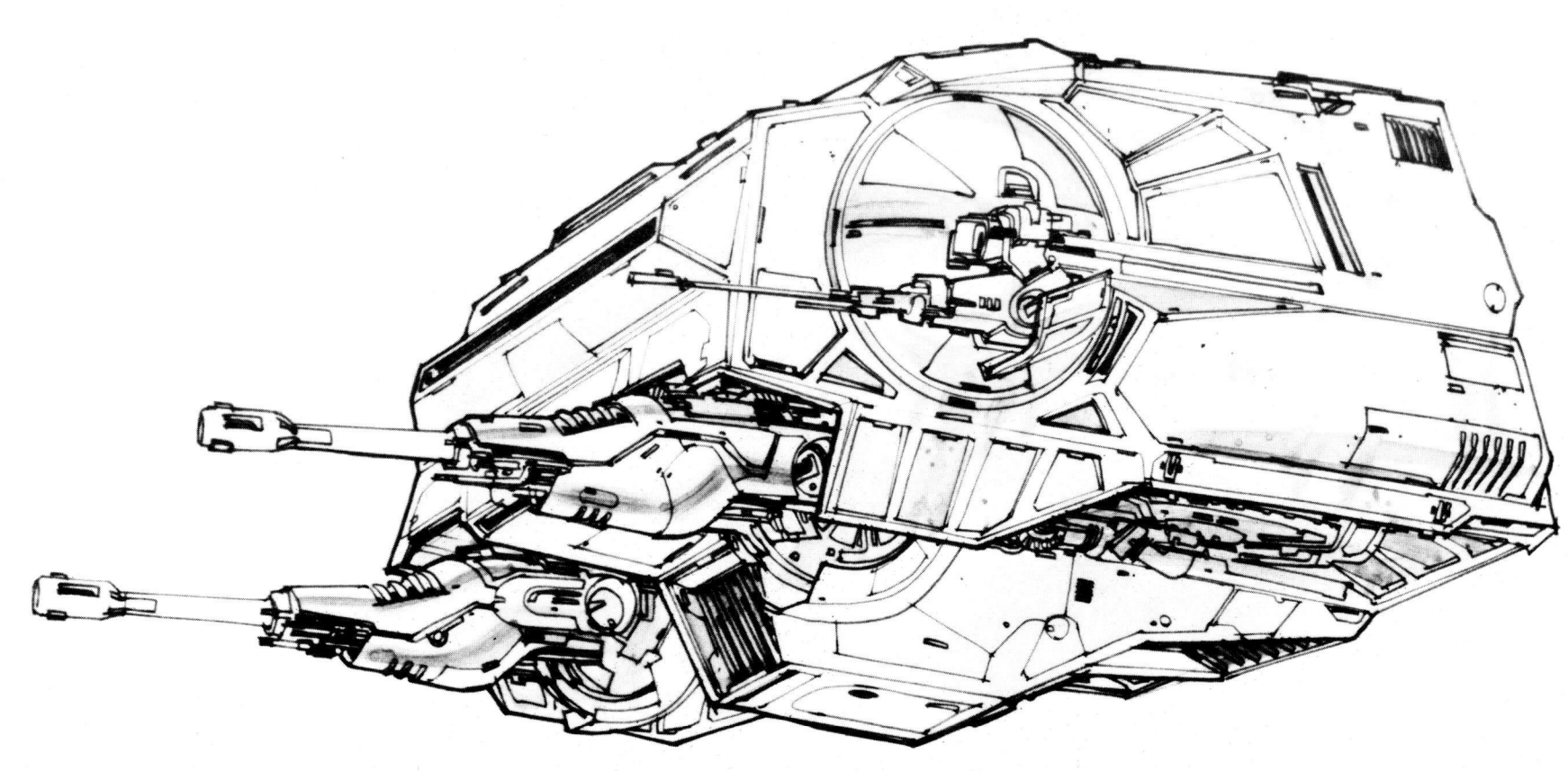

FINAL VERSION OF WALKER HEAD

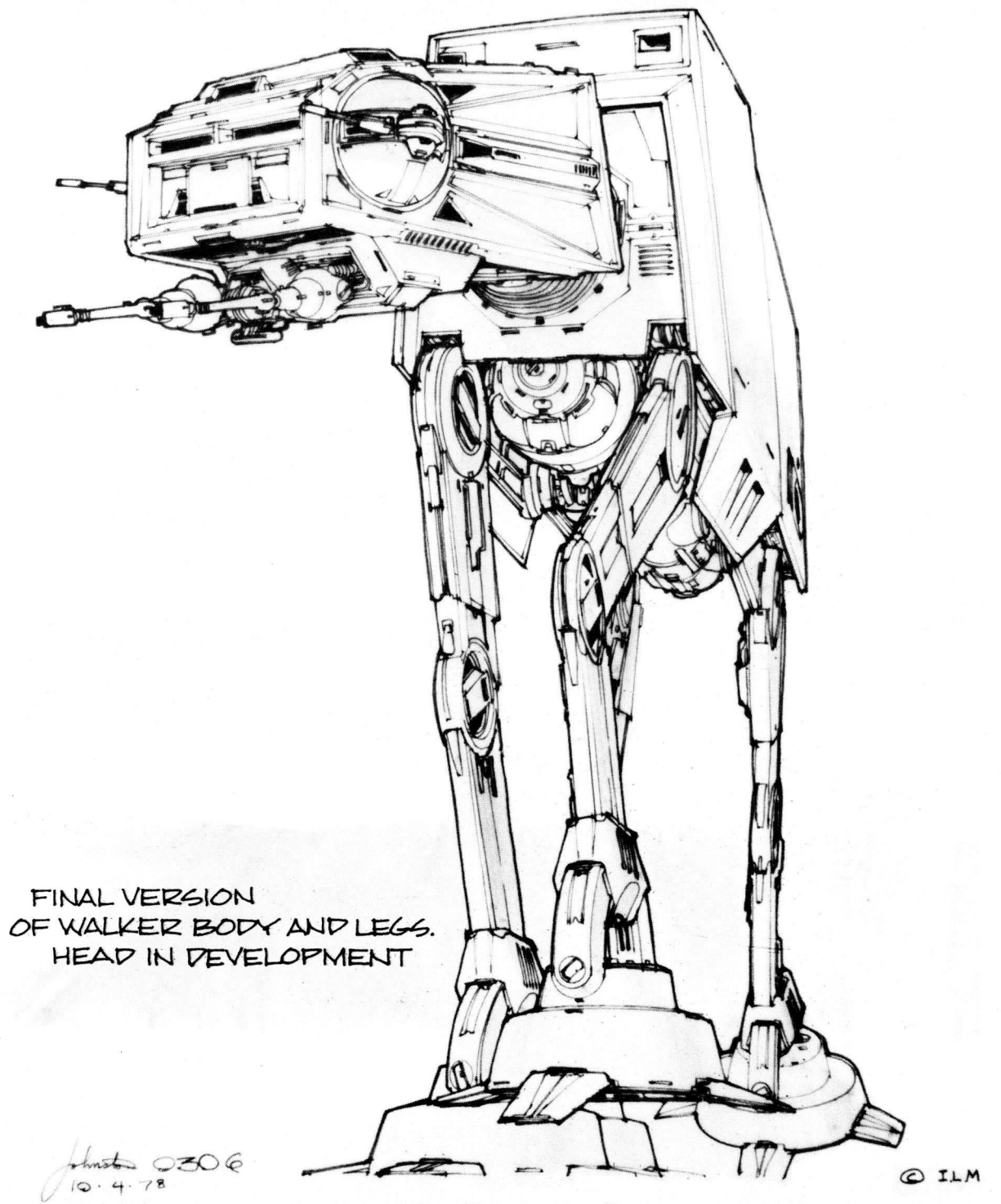

# SNOWTROOPER COSTUMES

Early designs for the snowtrooper outfits were based on the costumes of Japanese samurai warriors. This concept was dropped, and the artists used the basic stormtrooper costume to develop the look for the snowtroopers. An airtight fabric oversuit covers the troopers' armor for protection against the cold. To facilitate breathing in the bitter Hoth climate, a breather hood envelops the face plate and feeds into the suit liner.

EARLY IMPERIAL
SNOWTROOPER
OUTFIT SHOWING
JAPANESE INFLUENCE

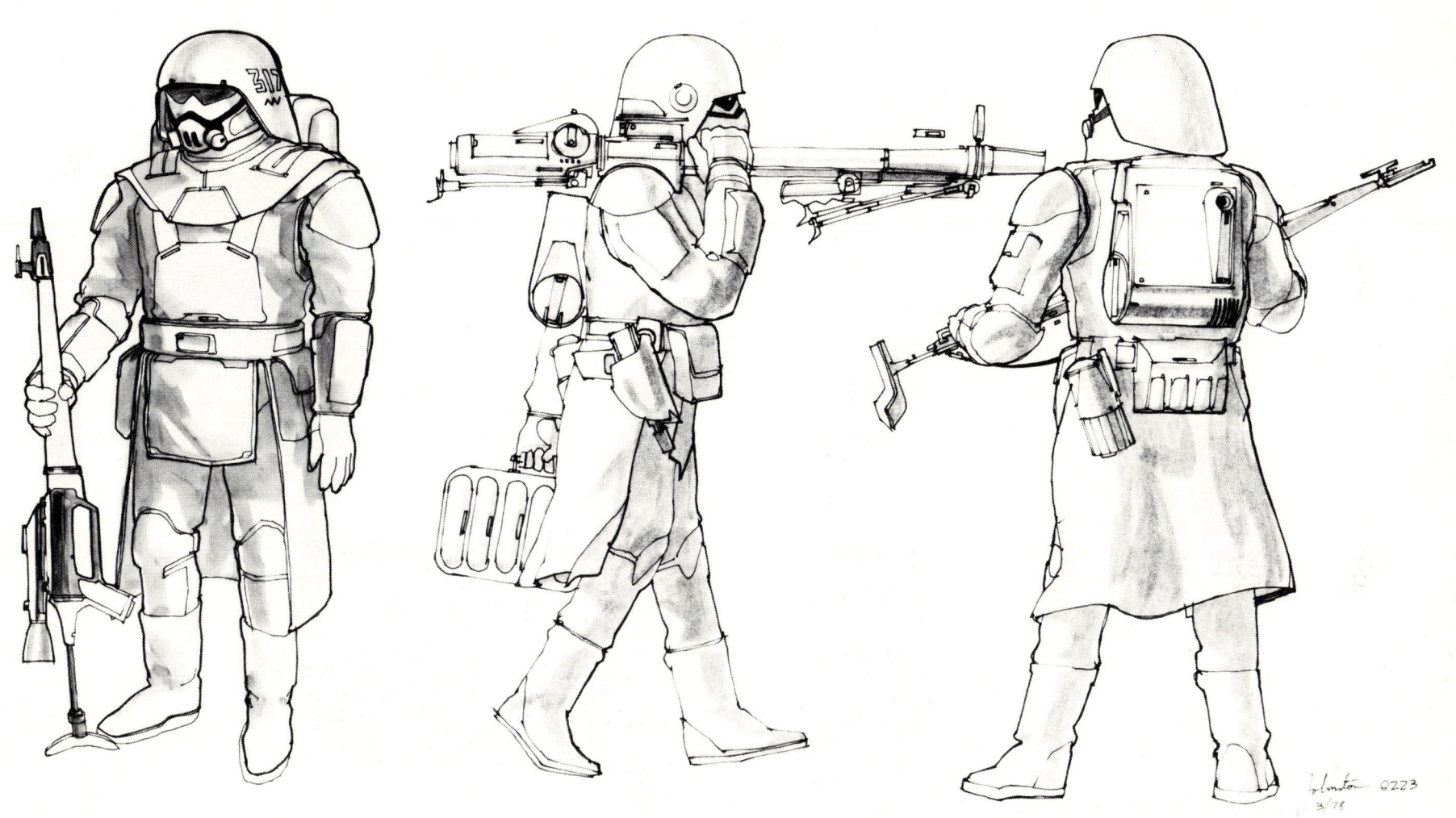

IMPERIAL SNOWTROOPER UNIFORMS AND WEAPONS

# TAUNTAUN

Originally the artists worked on designs that would have had a man wear the Tauntaun costume with a very small adult or a child as rider. But stop-motion animators Phil Tippett and Jon Berg convinced them that a highly detailed puppet could be used for most of the shots incorporating a Tauntaun, with a live-action head filling in for closeups. The final design for the Tauntaun seen in the film is Phil Tippett's.

VERY EARLY SKETCH FOR IMPERIAL TWO-LEGGED MOUNT, PRE-ICE PLANET

VERY EARLY SKETCH FOR IMPERIAL TWO-LEGGED MOUNT ON ICE PLANET

# YODA

In beginning the design process for Yoda, the artists knew only that he was to appear very, very old and have nonhuman characteristics. While some of the early Yoda sketches depict the little Jedi as more animal than human, in later stages the character became smaller, more wrinkled, and more gnomelike.

The artists' primary task in creating the Yoda design was to present the sculptors with a guideline from which to further develop the character. Working from this basic guideline, the sculptors were able to add personality and emotion to Yoda.

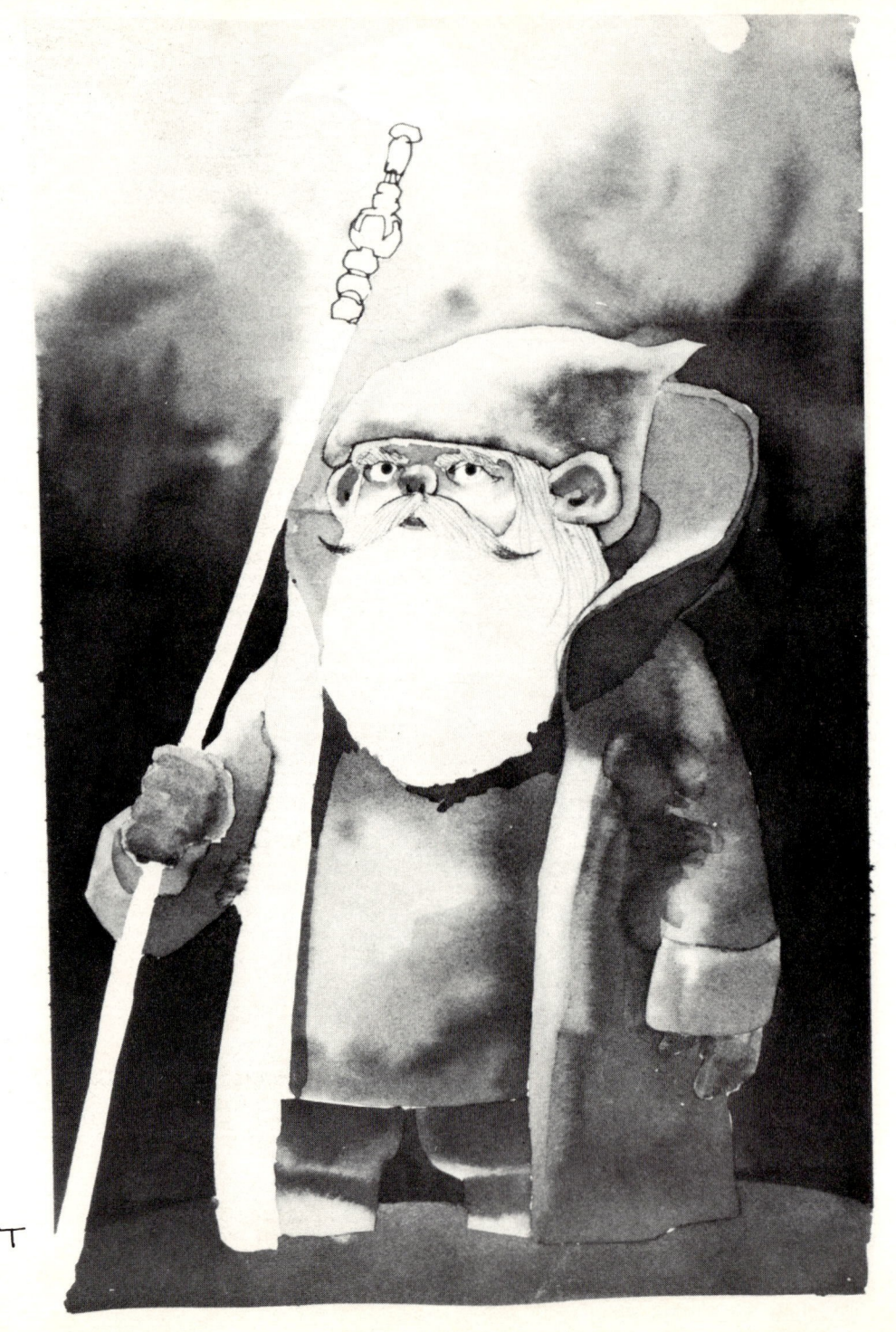

EARLY YODA CONCEPT

DEVELOPMENTAL YODA DESIGN

FINAL YODA HEAD DESIGN

FINAL YODA DESIGN

18"

THE EMPIRE STRIKES BACK SKETCHBOOK

# DARTH VADER'S STAR DESTROYER, EXECUTOR

As befits Vader's propensity for things malevolent, his special-edition Star Destroyer is larger, more evil-looking, and far more destructive than the other Star Destroyers in the Imperial fleet. The original concept was based on the idea of a "souped-up" version of the basic Star Destroyer ship as designed by the same manufacturer. The design evolved into a wider, larger, and sleeker version based on the original "arrowhead" shape. With its upper surface resembling a metropolitan skyline both in size and shape, Vader's ship sets him apart from the rest of the Imperial forces—for his is the latest and fastest model available.

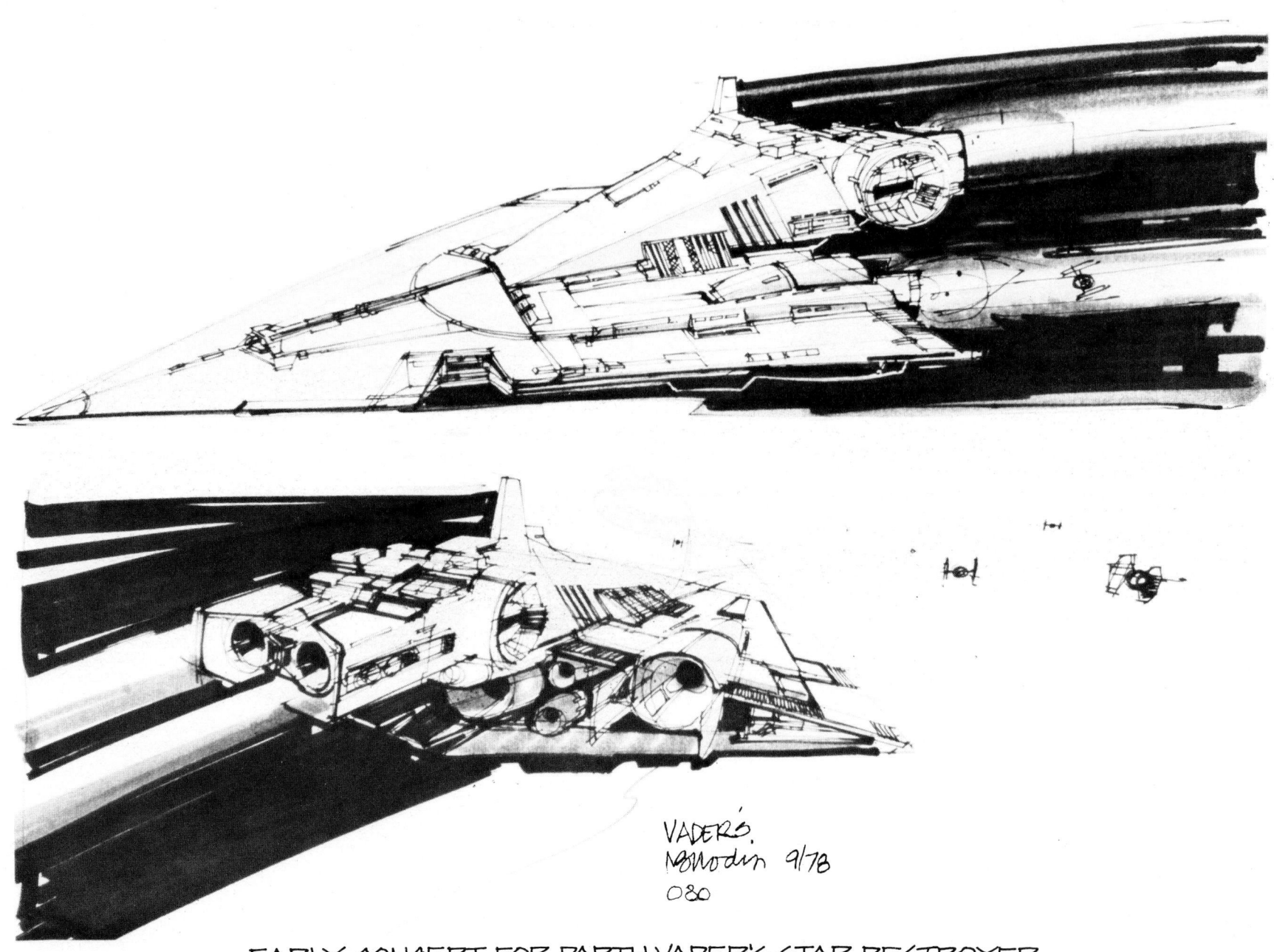

EARLY CONCEPT FOR DARTH VADER'S STAR DESTROYER, TIE FIGHTERS IN BACKGROUND

DARTH VADER'S STAR DESTROYER, SIDE VIEW

# REBEL CRUISER

George Lucas suggested that the design for the Rebel Cruiser be based on an elongated outboard motor shape. With this in mind, and with the goal of arriving at a unique but practical design, Johnston and Rodis-Jamero both worked on developing the final concept for the vast Rebel ship.

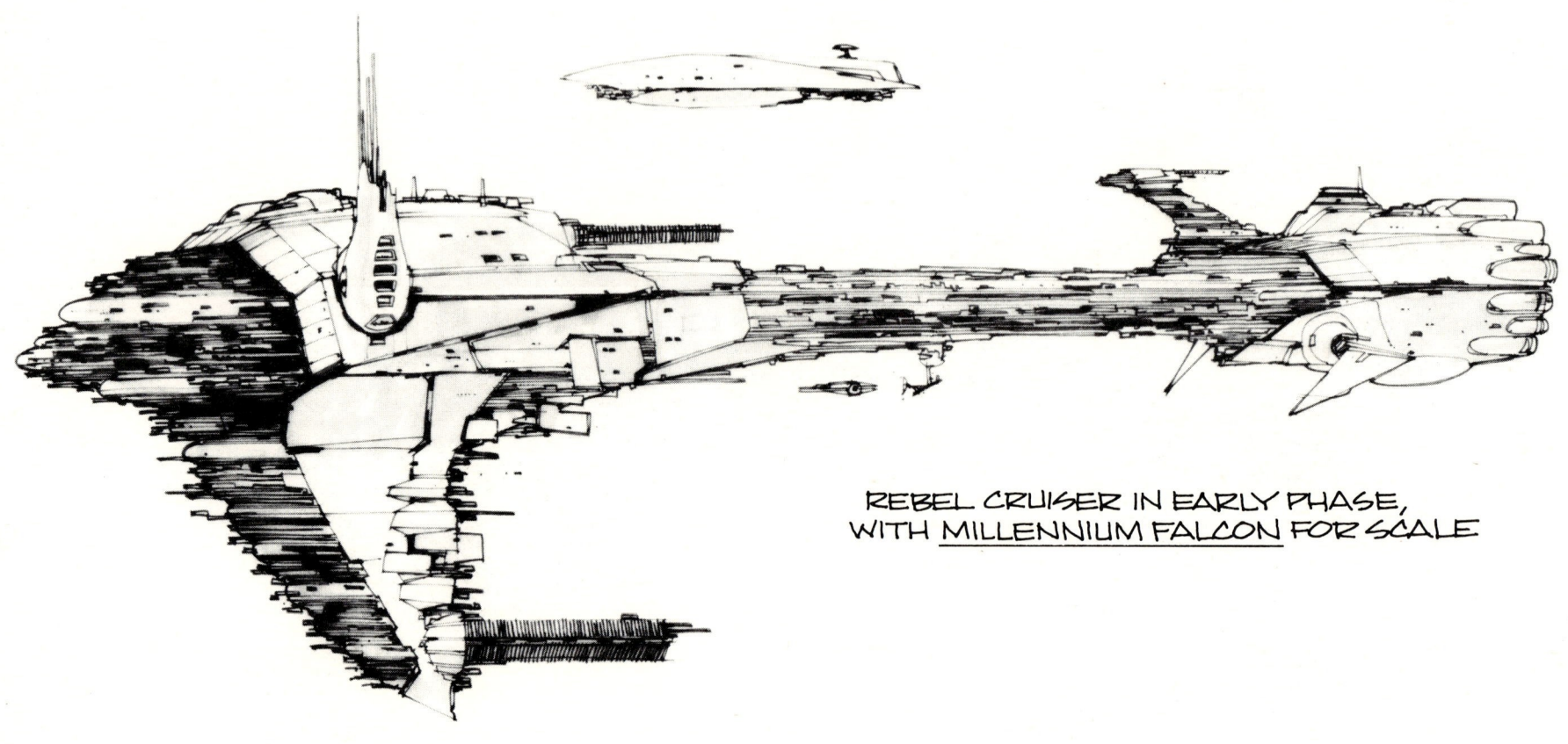

REBEL CRUISER IN EARLY PHASE, WITH MILLENNIUM FALCON FOR SCALE

# REBEL TRANSPORT

Converted from enormous space liners, the Rebel Transport ships have been hollowed out to make room for cargo containers. These vast carriers also contain passenger pods which serve to hold the large numbers of Rebel troops the ships must transport. Because the Rebel Transports are completely unarmed, they must rely on their X-wing fighter escort to protect them from Imperial attack.

rebel transport in ice hangar - Hoth

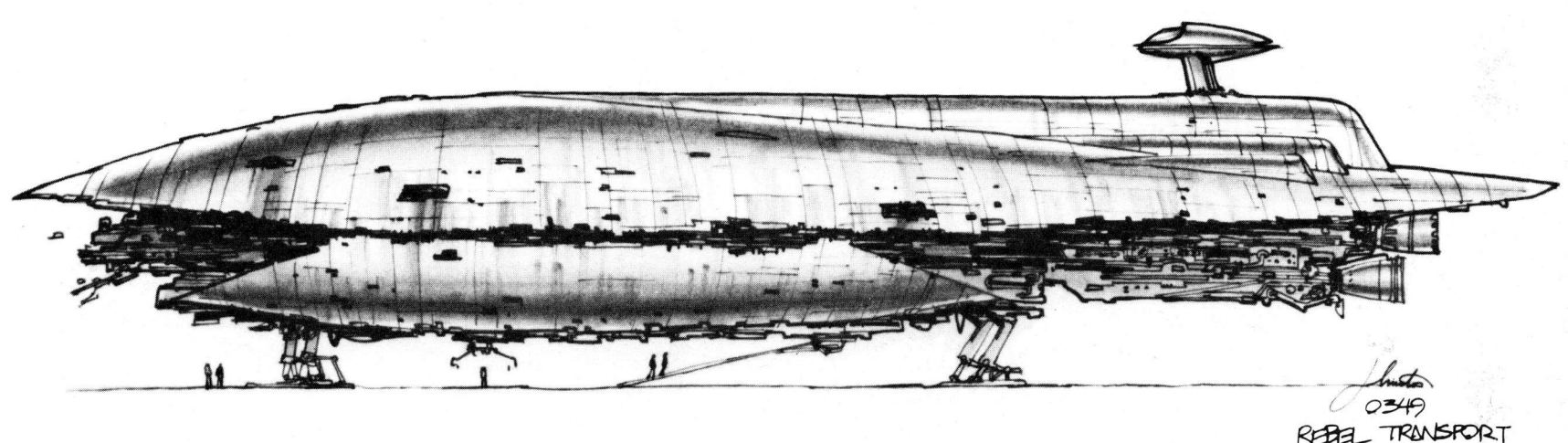

# BOBA FETT

While most of the film's costume design originated in England, Ralph McQuarrie and Johnston designed the Boba Fett outfit at Industrial Light and Magic in California. The costume was built at EMI in London, and then shipped back to Johnston to be painted. Originally the Boba Fett costume was intended to be worn by a squad of supercommandos, troops from the Mandalore system armed with weapons built into their suits. But the costume was adapted for the Boba Fett character by aging, denting, and adding a colorful paint job to one of these suits, while keeping the wrist lasers, flying backpack, and rocket darts originally intended for the supercommandos.

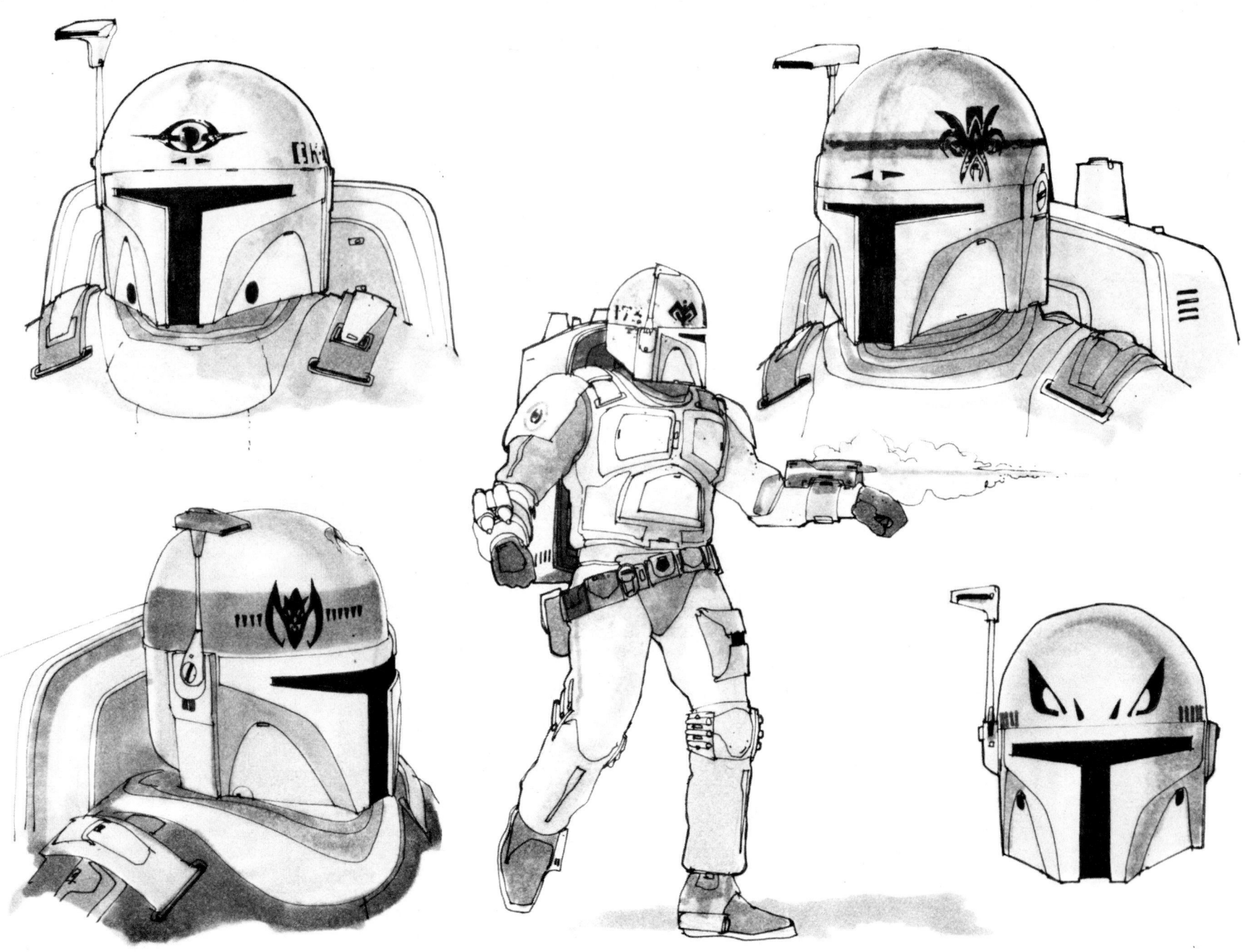

GRAPHIC IDEAS FOR
BOBA FETT'S HELMET AND SUIT

EARLY SKETCHES OF ARMORED SUIT FOR SUPERCOMMANDO.
LATER BECAME BOBA FETT.

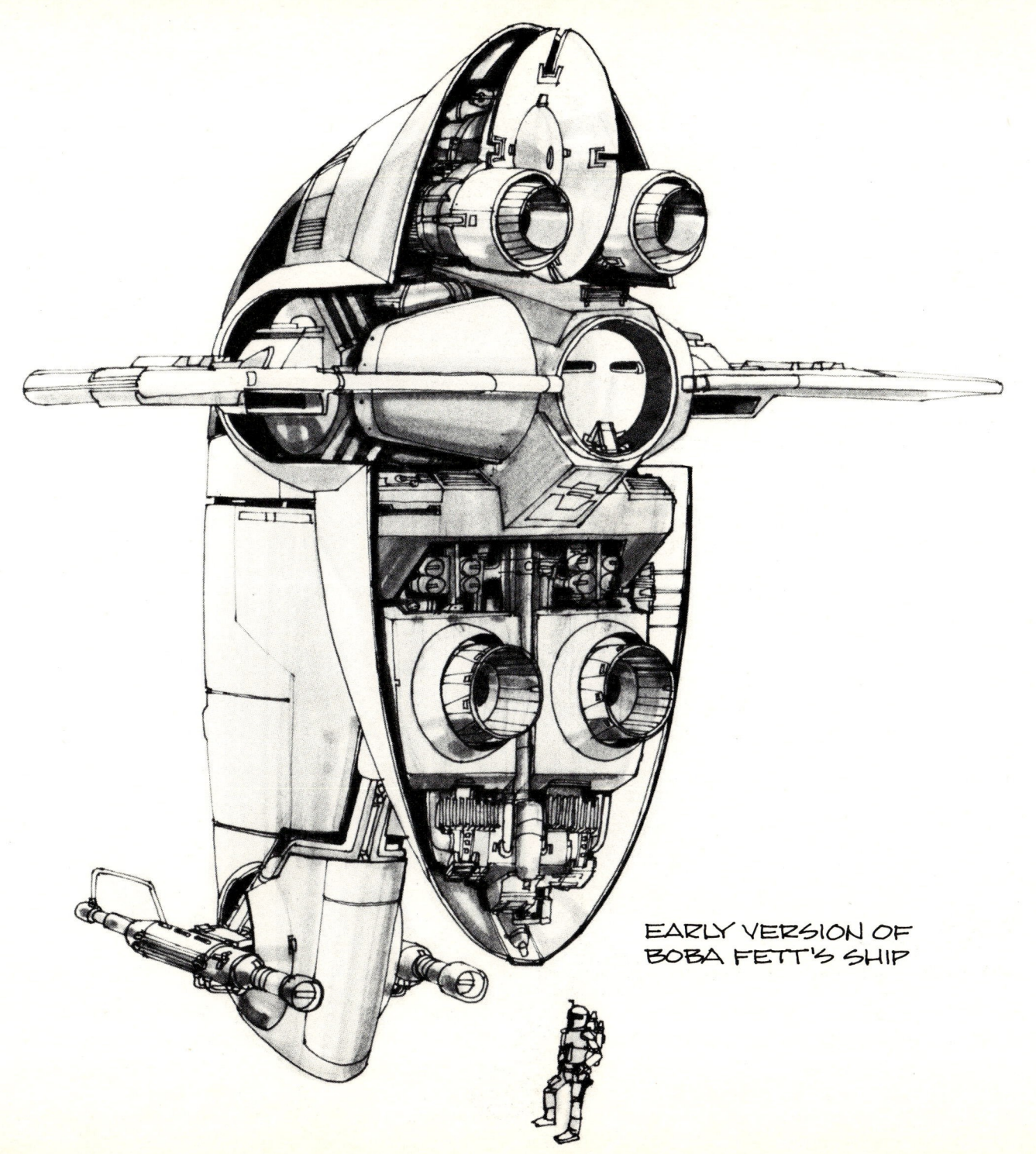

EARLY VERSION OF BOBA FETT'S SHIP

**LOADING RAMP AND DOOR ON BOBA FETT'S SHIP**

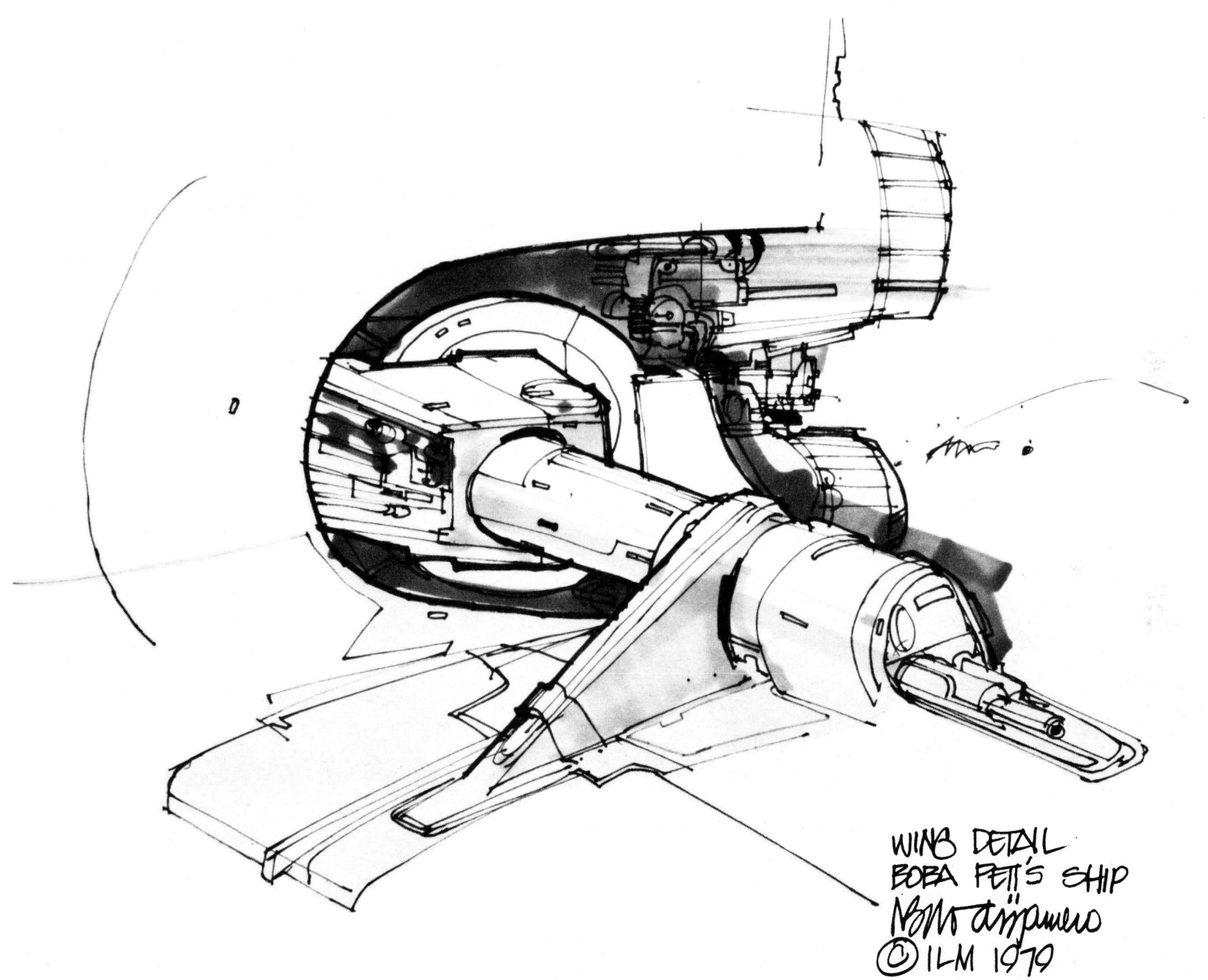

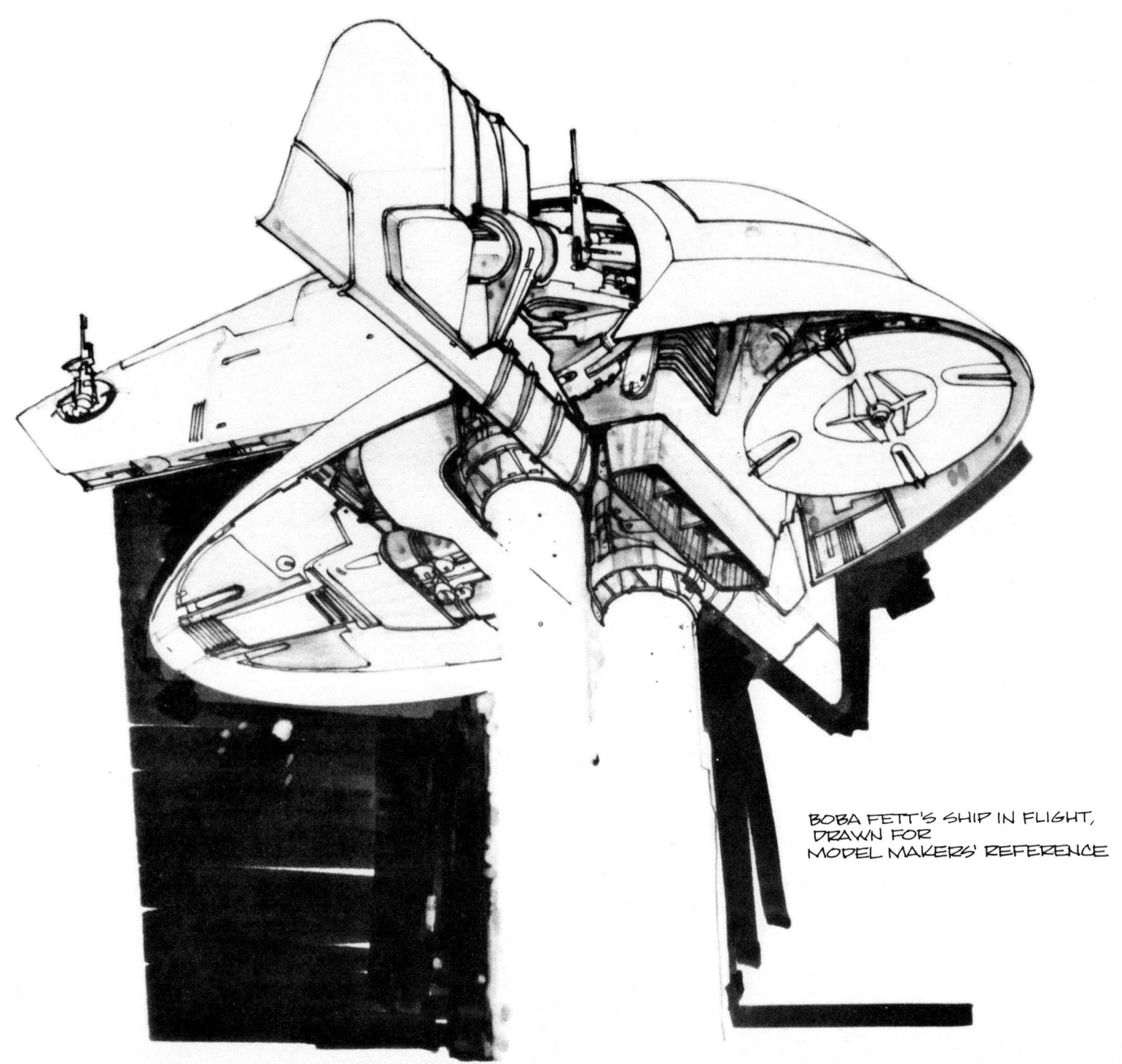

BOBA FETT'S SHIP IN FLIGHT, DRAWN FOR MODEL MAKERS' REFERENCE

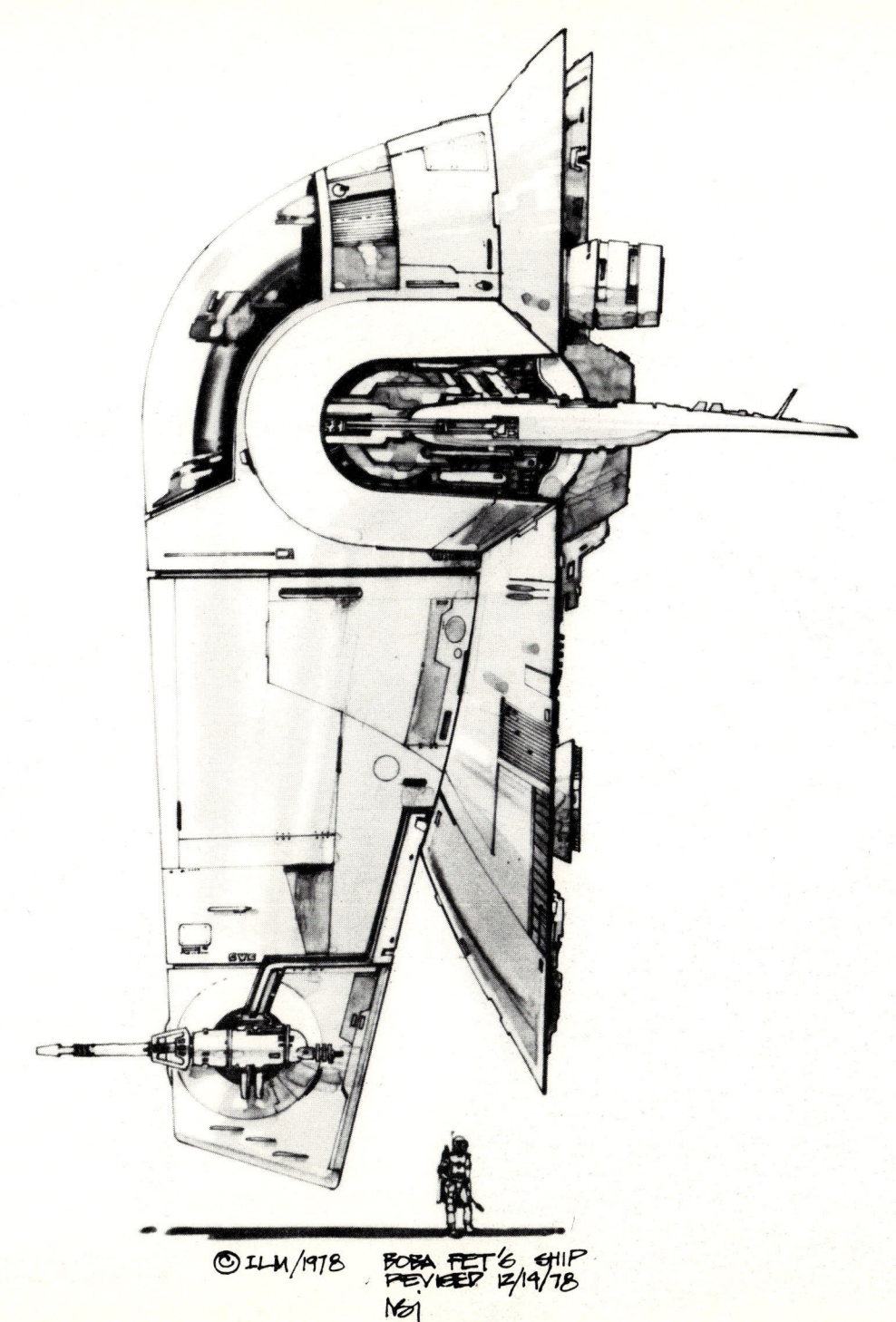

# CLOUD CITY ARCHITECTURE

The 1930s period of design influenced the artists in conceptualizing Cloud City. Their designs picked up the streamline aspects, curved lines, and modernistic elements characteristic of that era. The artists incorporated the basic look of a metropolis of the future with believable and seemingly practical building designs.

The Cloud City skyline was achieved by filming models that were based on the artists' designs against a matte painting backdrop.

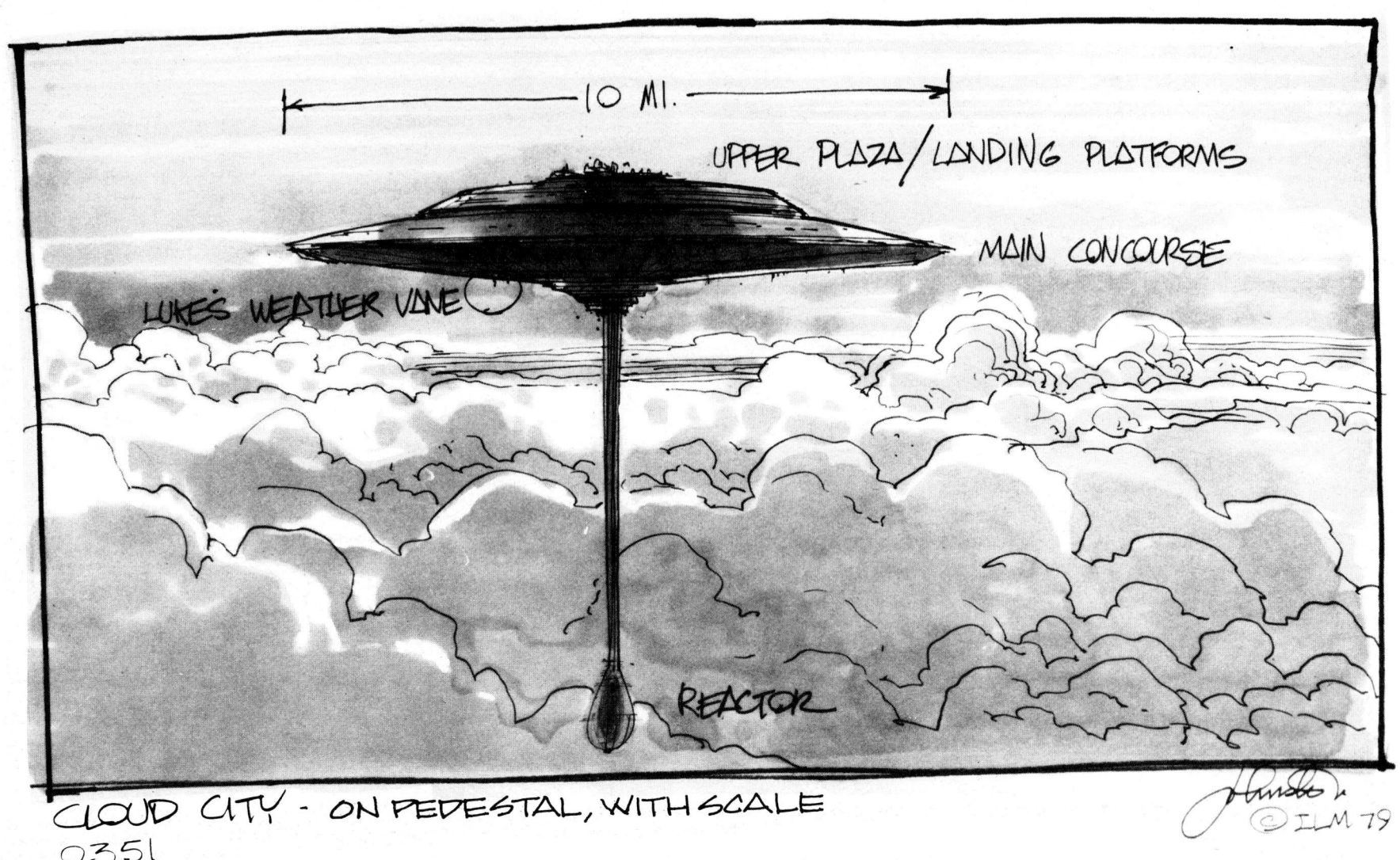

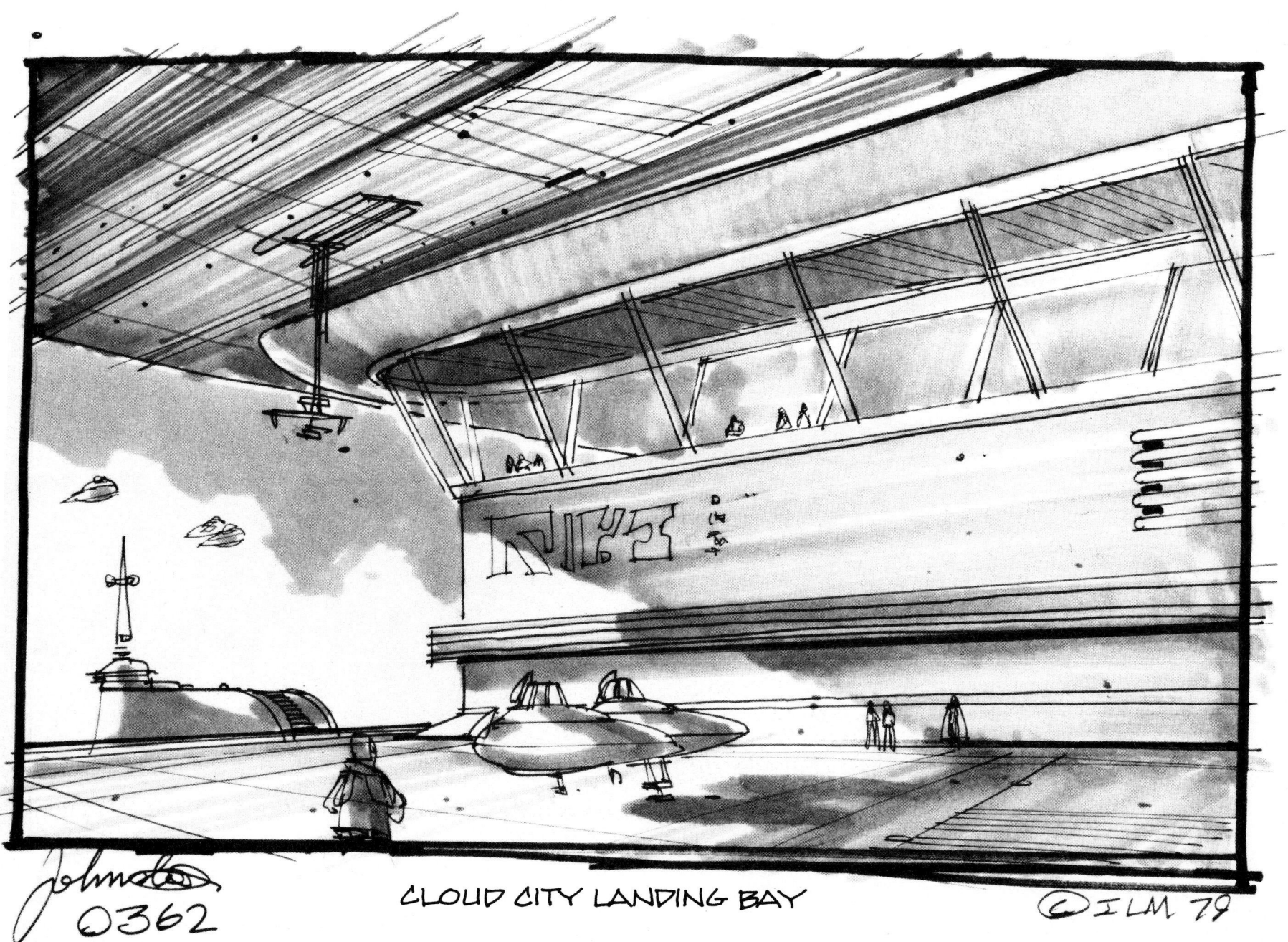
CLOUD CITY LANDING BAY

cloud city / main concourse

cloud car landing platform

0359    CLOUD CITY PLAZA

# TWIN-POD CLOUD CAR

Just as automobiles are used on earth, so are cloud cars used on the Cloud City of Bespin. Although only one version of the cloud car is shown here, the designs could be adapted to suit the needs of a patrol craft, pleasure car, personal transportation, or other type of vehicle. The shape of these flying cars was strongly influenced by the Streamline era of design which is reflected in the general architecture and look of Cloud City.

EARLY DEVELOPMENTAL SKETCH OF SINGLE-POD CLOUD CAR

EARLY DEVELOPMENTAL SKETCH OF TWIN-POD CLOUD CAR

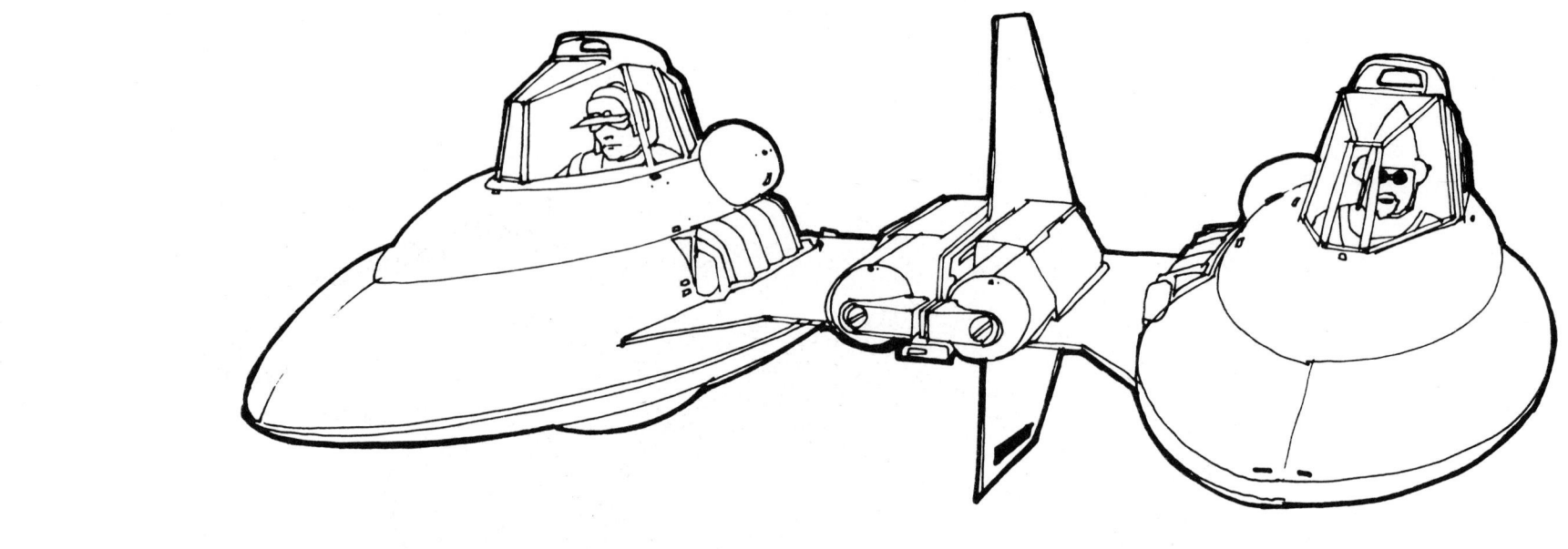

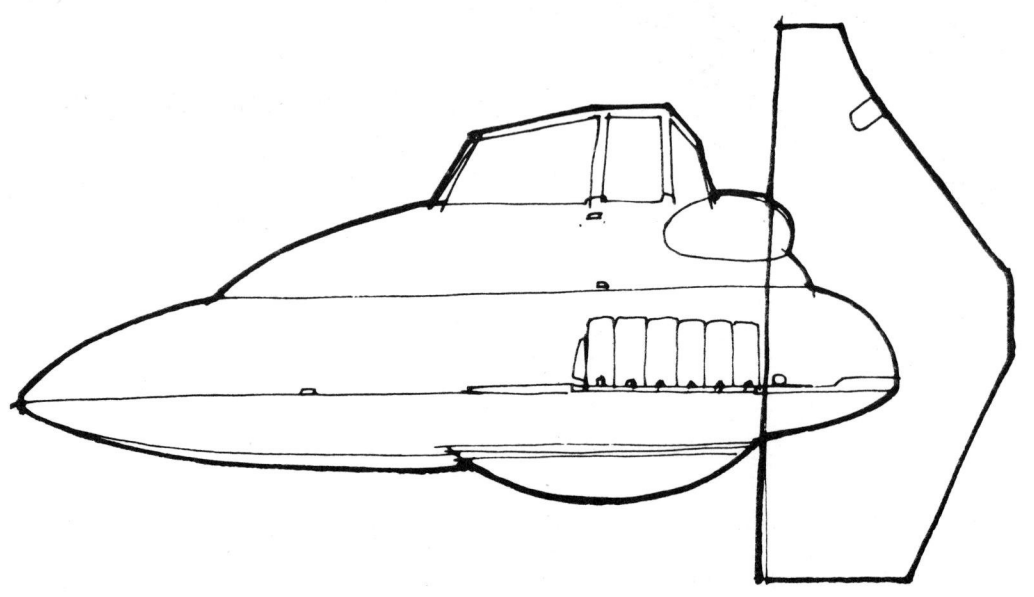

CLOUD CAR
WITH STEERING VANE FEATURED

JEJ 0065
12/77

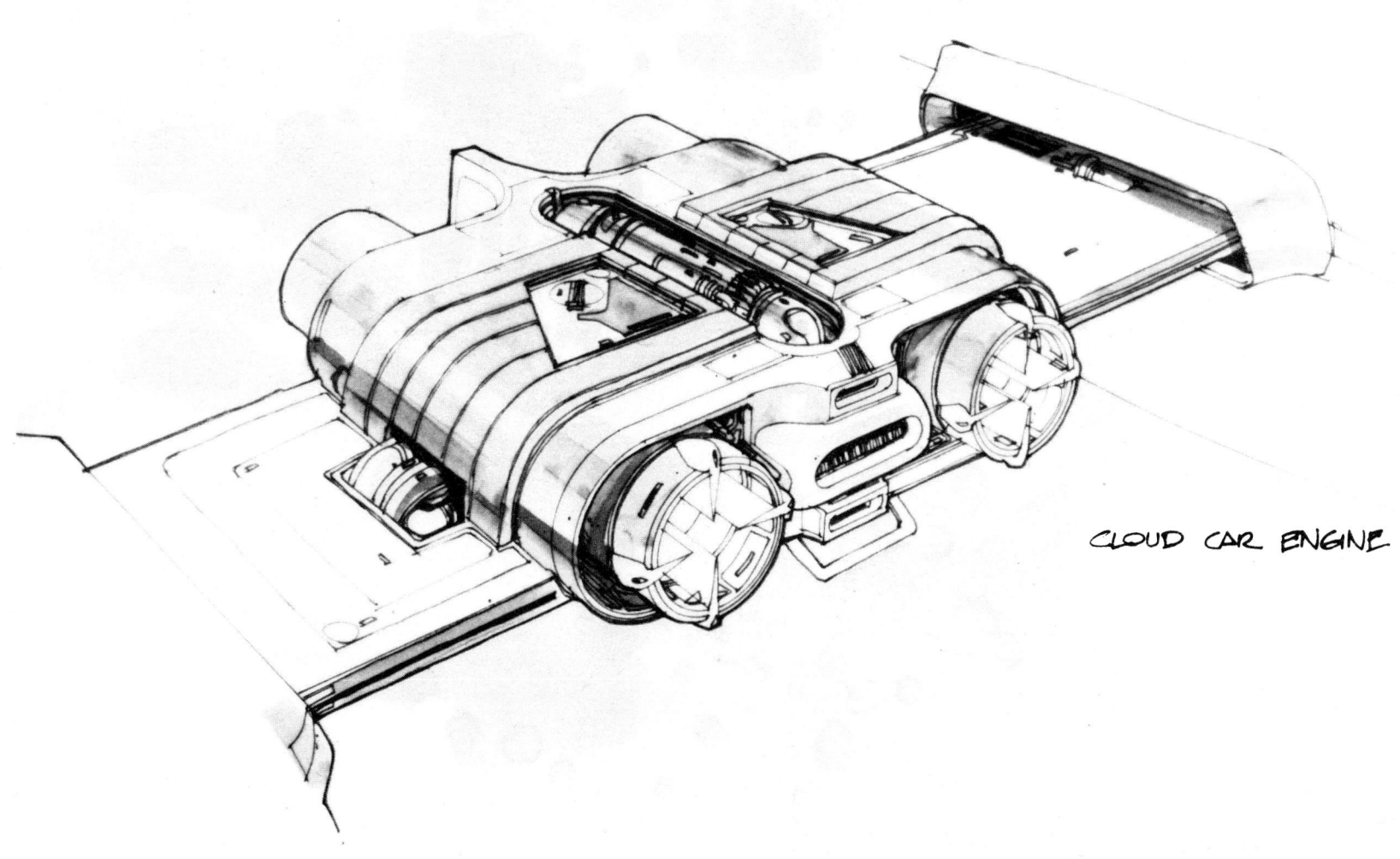

CLOUD CAR ENGINE

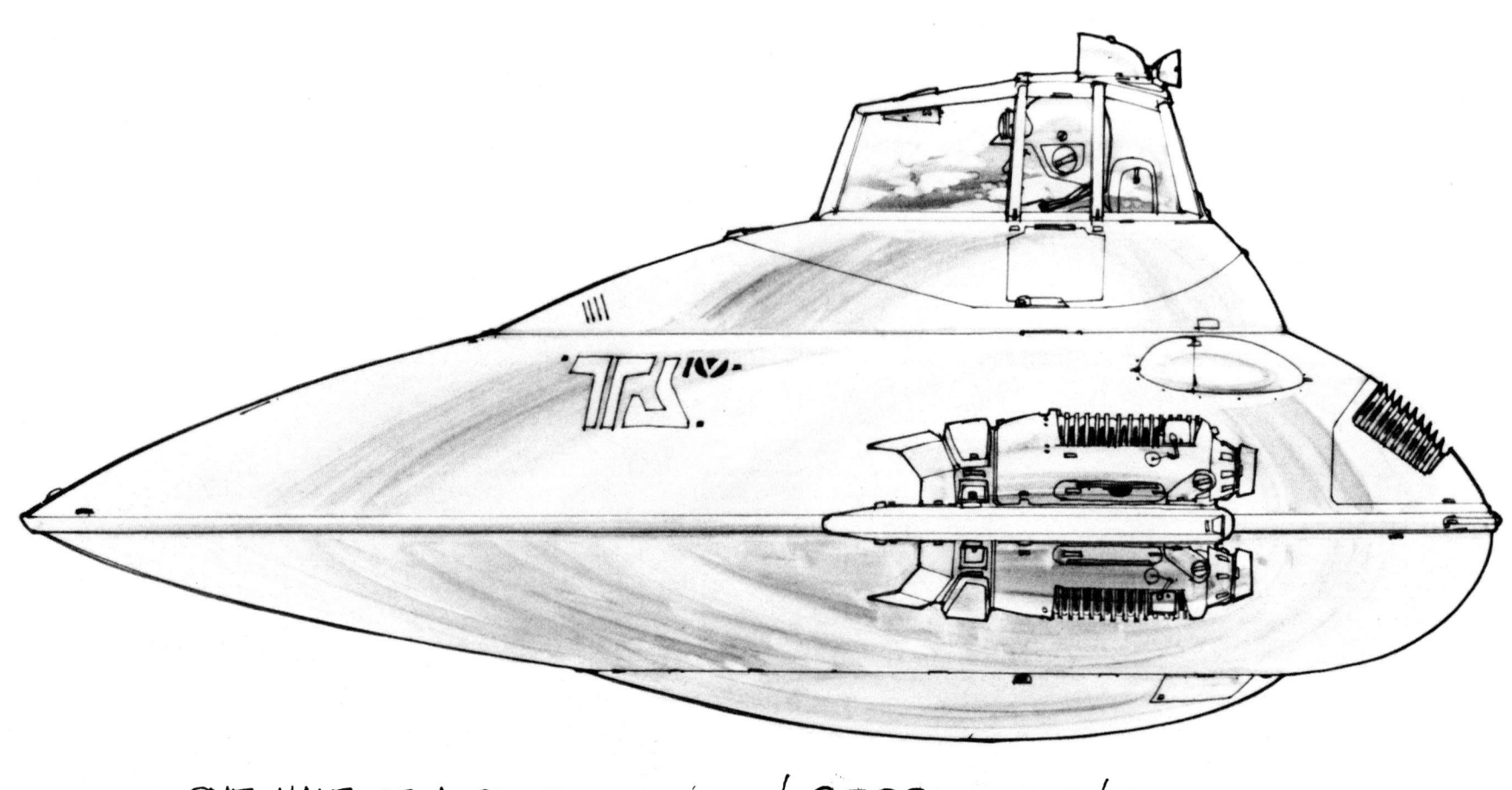

ONE-HALF OF A CLOUD CAR   0308   8/78

CLOUD CAR WITH LANDING GEAR EXTENDED